A WHOLE LIFE

MY PATH FROM HARD-TIME KID TO
HIGH-IMPACT CONSULTANT

Copyright © 2024 by Jack Jameson

Published by Four Rivers Media

All rights reserved. No portion of this book may be reproduced, stored in a retrieval system, or transmitted in any form or by any means—electronic, mechanical, photocopy, recording, scanning, or other—except for brief quotations in critical reviews or articles, without prior written permission of the author.

Cover design by: Sara Young
Cover photo by: Andrew van Tilborgh

ISBN: 978-1-960678-78-2   1 2 3 4 5 6 7 8 9 10

Printed in the United States of America

JACK JAMESON

A WHOLE LIFE

MY PATH FROM HARD-TIME KID TO HIGH-IMPACT CONSULTANT

*To God and my beautiful wife, Kim.
I would not be the man I am today without
either of them. He set me on the right
path, and she is perfecting me....*

ACKNOWLEDGMENTS

Martijn van Tilborgh at Four Rivers Media: thanks for believing that I had a story worth sharing.

Andy Butcher, my collaborator: thank you for your patience with my accent and my funny words. And for having me dig deep into my soul, and for really listening and giving my story direction.

My "M&M" children—Mark, Megan, Marcie, Mason, Madison: I am blessed to be your father and grateful for the love and support you give me. I love you more than words can express.

Joseph Bertagnole (Dad): I am so grateful to you for being my mentor and the father I never had. Thank you for trusting me with your precious daughter. Can't wait to see you again one day.

Darnell Bertagnole (Mom): Thanks for inviting me to dinner for the best fried chicken in the world and always treating me as one of your own. I love you.

To all nine of my wife's brothers and sisters—thank you for accepting me as one of your own and being like real brothers and sisters to me.

Scott Stratton (and family): Thanks for being my best friend for so many years. You and your family treated me as a brother and a son. So many of the good things I got to experience growing up were because of you and your family. I miss you, Scott. Looking forward to catching up one day in heaven.

My Farmers family: thanks for everlasting friendships and fun times. Thanks for the support from so many, too numerous to count. Once Farmers family, always Farmers family.

CONTENTS

Acknowledgments vii
Introduction 11
Chapter 1 15
Chapter 2 23
Chapter 3 35
Chapter 4 43
Chapter 5 53
Chapter 6 61
Chapter 7 71
Chapter 8 79
Chapter 9 89
Chapter 10 99
Chapter 11 107
Chapter 13 125
Chapter 14 135
Chapter 15 145
Chapter 16 157
Chapter 17 167
Chapter 18 177
Chapter 19 185
Chapter 20 195
Chapter 21 205
Afterword 217
About the Author 227

INTRODUCTION

My wife, Kim, wanted to know why I hadn't told her about Jeffrey.

"Jeffrey who?" I asked.

"Jeffrey your half-brother," she said.

"I don't have a half-brother called Jeffrey."

"Yes, you do," Kim said.

In the few years we had been married, we'd never found ourselves as confused with each other as this. We traded baffled looks.

"Why do you think I have a half-brother called Jeffrey?" I asked.

"Because your mom just told me," Kim said.

Apparently, during a visit to see Kim and me and our toddler daughters, the two of them had been chatting about family while I was out at work. During the conversation, Mom let slip that she'd had a son I knew nothing about. Jeffrey had been the result of a brief liaison, and he had been given up to be raised by another family before I was born.

You might think such a revelation would up-end your world, but for me, this discovery was just another twist in a tangled family history. Another chapter in a pretty crazy story.

It's been said that home should be a refuge from the storms of life, but what do you do when it seems to be the center of them instead? I was the sixth of my mother's nine children, three of whom (including Jeffrey) I didn't know about when I was a kid. My father may have been the third of her possibly five husbands, and he had two and possibly more other children I knew nothing about for the longest time. As you can tell, there was a high level of uncertainty about much of my childhood.

Not surprisingly, then, for as long as I can remember, when I was growing up, it seemed like I was stepping into some kind of family drama whenever I opened the front door and went inside. It almost felt like I needed to take a deep breath as I plunged into deep waters.

And then there was an ever-changing cast of characters. Siblings that came and went. Relatives on parole, on the run, or on the prowl. Several men who filled the space of an absent father to a minor degree for different seasons and a series of others who passed through as though our house was an extension of the local bar. The only constant presence through all of this was my mom, the apparently still center around which all the other chaos seemed to swirl, even as she was actually the source of much of it.

I may not know all the backstories of some of the incidents in my childhood, but what happened remains indelibly in my memory. When you live in confusion, you develop a heightened sense of awareness, a hyper-alertness that enables you to take in what's happening around you in detail because being vigilant and spotting those small things may be essential to your safety.

While I can vividly recall so many situations and scenes, they don't come with tremendous emotional pain. Some sadness and regret, on occasions, for sure, but nothing that weighs me down.

In some ways, those experiences seem to belong to another person whom I got to observe.

And that's actually why I'm sharing my story. Not to throw anyone under the bus or to have anyone feel sorry for me. I know many people have experienced more difficult things than me. Rather, I am writing to share hope and joy. Because even though I endured some difficult times, my past has not restricted my present, and I am confident it won't limit my future. I've enjoyed a rich and meaningful life not so much in defiance of my past but to some measure because of it, and the things that I learned about myself and others as a result.

I hope that in reading, you will be encouraged to believe that, whatever your circumstances, you can rise above them. No matter what hard things you may have had to go through, you have made it this far! And if you're willing to let go of the past, seize hold of the opportunities that come your way, and give them your best shot—there's nothing to hold you back.

CHAPTER 1

I was eight or nine years old when I met my father for the first time. By Mom's telling, she had divorced Jackie Wayne Blankenship when she was around seven months pregnant with me, and he went to jail for some petty crime stuff. It wasn't his first spell inside, and it wouldn't be his last.

Prior to our meeting, I had heard from Dad just once, when I was small. He sent me a children's picture book from prison, *That's What Friends Are For*.[1] It seems like an odd gift to send your son, but maybe there wasn't an extensive selection in the commissary. Or perhaps he didn't feel he'd been enough of a father figure to choose something more familial. "To Jackie Wayne," he wrote in it. "From daddy. I love you, son."

I don't know whether Dad thought I'd been named after him, but strangely enough, that wasn't the case. When I arrived at Dallas' Parkland Hospital on April 28, 1965, eighteen months after President John F. Kennedy was pronounced dead there following his shooting, Mom let my half-brothers Jack and Garry choose my names. Jack picked Jackie, while Garry went for Wayne, his middle name.

Other than that one gift, until he made contact out of the blue asking to see me, I had never heard anything much about my

---
[1] Florence Parry Heidi, *That's What Friends Are For* (Somerville, MA: Candlewick, 2007).

father. Mom never really talked about him, never suggested I write to him in prison, and somehow, I knew not to ask her about him. The closest I ever got to him in any sense was visiting his mother once when I was maybe four or five. That in itself was unusual because Mom had maintained a little bit of contact with her ex-mother-in-law even though, typically, when she moved on from a guy, he and his world were history.

Mom said my paternal grandmother was always very loving toward her, and when I pressed her about Dad when I was older, Mom, unusually for her, found it hard to say anything really negative about him. She recalled that he always treated her well, especially compared to Tony, her first husband. She just couldn't put up with his running around and his laziness, she said; he preferred trying to make easy money rather than holding down a steady job.

Pretty much everyone I have spoken to in my wider family seemed to like him. They have told me how he was easygoing and charming, always the life of the party. Good-looking and confident, with a sharp sense of humor, he had a talent for working a room.

Given the positive impression he could make on people, I have wondered why I never heard from him for so long. Did I just not matter to him? Was that friendliness all just part of his thing, his way of getting what he wanted from people? Or did he feel bad about going to prison, that somehow he wasn't a good example to his son?

Whatever the reason for those long years of silence, I was over the moon when Mom told me he wanted to see me for a weekend. I was going to spend some time with my dad! I bragged about it to all of my friends. When he asked me what I wanted to do, I told him that I'd never stayed in a hotel and I really wanted to, so he said fine. Only, true to form, things weren't so straightforward when he came to pick me up in his car.

First, I got introduced to his current girlfriend, Laura. She was friendly, but she didn't know much about how to interact with kids, apparently—her conversational gambit was to show me the photo album she used to book her gigs as a stripper. I don't know what made my young eyes go wider, seeing pictures of her scantily clad ample body or of the boa constrictor she'd trained to provide strategic, slithery cover.

Because we lived on a regular diet of bologna, beans, and cornbread at home, my weekend-with-Dad wish list also included dining out at an all-you-can-eat shrimp restaurant. It was a great first evening together—until Dad told me he had to leave. Apparently, as part of his latest prison release, he was residing at a halfway house with a nighttime curfew. That left Laura and me alone at the hotel together—in separate beds, thankfully, and equally thankfully, without her snake. Not many third graders can brag about having a sleepover with their father's stripper girlfriend.

The next day, we all hung out together. We went to the park, and then Dad took me to a toy store, where he told me I could choose something. I hardly ever got new toys because Mom's welfare money didn't go very far, so to be able to select whatever I wanted was beyond special. A huge fan of *Planet of the Apes*—I never missed either the TV series[2] or the movies[3], whenever they re-ran—I picked out an action figure playset that I treasured for years.

---
2 *Planet of the Apes*, Arnold Laven, et. al. (September 13, 1974: CBS), Television.
3 Franklin J. Schaffner, *Planet of the Apes* (February 8, 1968; Hollywood, CA: APJAC Productions).

Come evening, Dad had to go back to the halfway house again, but this time, Laura wasn't on babysitting duty. We visited Dad's sister, who lived in the area, and I spent the night there. She had a daughter about my age, nicknamed Punkin, and we enjoyed playing together. The following morning, Dad came to collect me, and with Laura, we ate out again—this time a hearty breakfast at a local Sambo's.

Driving home, my stomach and my heart were full. Dad had fed me well and bought me a gift I treasured—but more importantly, I'd had his attention and his affection. I mattered to him. "We'll do this again, okay?" he told me when he dropped me back at Mom's. I couldn't wait, wondering each time when the phone rang whether that was him calling to arrange our next visit.

I never heard from him again.

Over time, I learned to tuck my disappointment away and accept that was just the way things were. But every time I played with his gift or watched *Planet of the Apes*,[4] I'd remember that weekend with a sense of wonder and regret.

If I've learned one thing in life, it's that speculation gets you nowhere. Spending too much time trying to work out why people do the things they do—or don't do them—isn't helpful. Still, to this day, some part of me wants to give Dad the benefit of the doubt for never following up with me. So, I wonder if he tried to make contact, but maybe it was one of those times we didn't have a phone? Or perhaps he went back to jail again and thought I'd be better off without him in my life?

---

4 Schaffner, *Planet of the Apes*.

My one lingering regret is that I don't have the one photo I know of the two of us together. His sister snapped it during our visit and later sent it to Mom, who showed it to me. I can still see it in my mind's eye; we're sitting close together in a recliner, just me and my dad. He's smiling, and I am looking content.

> **IF I'VE LEARNED ONE THING IN LIFE, IT'S THAT SPECULATION GETS YOU NOWHERE. SPENDING TOO MUCH TIME TRYING TO WORK OUT WHY PEOPLE DO THE THINGS THEY DO— OR DON'T DO THEM—ISN'T HELPFUL.**

Everyone who knew him says how similar we are in many ways. We share the same dark complexion, and I like to think I got at least a smidgen of his good looks! One of my aunts says how similar our personalities are, and I wonder if I inherited a portion of his outgoing nature. She has told me it's scary how much I remind her of him, even down to some mannerisms I would have no way of copying. It makes me feel proud, in a way. Though I don't have a lot of memories of him, I'm glad that people speak positively of him and of what they see of him in me.

I was married with a family of my own when I learned Dad had died some years previously. No one from his family had ever reached out to let me know, which makes me wonder how many of them even knew about me. The story I heard was that he'd contracted AIDS while in prison and had been released for the last few months of his life.

I've never felt the need to dig for all the details of his life, though I have found some information online that confirms his lengthy criminal history. In 1991, I learned that he unsuccessfully appealed a twenty-year sentence for drug trafficking. Part of the reason it was so long is that when he was arrested, he was in possession of a .357 magnum despite being barred from owning a firearm for what court documents call "three prior violent felonies." Those files also refer to previous convictions for burglary dating back to 1959 and 1962, long before I arrived.

After I heard of his passing, I tracked down a photo of his headstone online, which brought me a sense of finality. No point wishing and wondering what might have been anymore. The little boy in me needn't wait any longer for a call.

With no consistent father figure in my life, Mom was the center of my world. I longed for her attention, affection, and affirmation, but she seemed elusive much of the time, somewhere beyond my reach. Maybe it was because she had grown up learning that the world was a dangerous place, and it wasn't wise to get too close to people.

A sharecropper's daughter, Evelyn Black was born during the Depression. According to family lore, her grandfather was raised by Choctaw Indians after they raided his family's farm, killing everyone but him. He then married a full-blooded Choctaw woman. Mom told me how her education ended in the sixth grade when she was sent out into the fields in Baskin, Louisiana, to pick cotton. Her father told her she was more useful there than sitting in school. It was a hardscrabble life, working all day in the hot sun. Things didn't get any easier when she went home; her father mistreated Mom and her four siblings. Their mother sometimes tried to intervene when he was lashing out at them, putting herself between them and their father.

Mom didn't talk much about her early years, but she did recall one incident when she was in her teens that was especially traumatic. She'd gone with her oldest brother, Uncle Sonny, as I knew him, to the liquor store and was sitting in the car while he went inside. As she was waiting, a man came up to the vehicle brandishing a knife and ordered her to get out. He steered her to another vehicle with two men inside and made her get in.

Pushing her down onto the floorboards, with one of them keeping her flat with his foot on her back, they drove away into the countryside. She could hear them talking about what they would do to her once they got her somewhere remote. She knew that she was going to be raped and killed. Thinking quickly, Mom called out that she felt sick, and they needed to stop, or she would throw up in the car. Her abductors pulled over to the side of the road and let her out, one of them holding her by her wrist as she bent over, pretending to retch. Somehow, she managed to break free and took off running down a dirt road, at the end of which, thankfully, was an old farmhouse.

When a man came and opened the door to her desperate banging, she threw herself into his arms. "Call the cops! Call the cops!" she screamed. "Those men kidnapped me. Please help."

One of the guys who had taken her came up to the door and told the man that Mom was crazy. "She's my wife, sir," he said.

"Sorry to disturb you; this kind of thing happens all the time. Please just give her back to me."

Fortunately, the man was suspicious enough to be uncertain. "I don't know what's going on here, so I'm just going to call the police and let them handle this, okay?" With that, my mom's abductors took off. Who knows what she escaped?

Along with what happened at home, that experience is the sort of thing that can shape your view of the world and men in particular. For Mom, it certainly seems to have had an impact—when it came to guys, she couldn't live without them but couldn't live with them, either.

At some stage, my grandfather moved the family to the Dallas area, where he started a construction business. With life at home so difficult, Mom escaped as early as she could, but it turned out to be jumping from the frying pan into the fire. Her first marriage, to Tony, lasted seven or eight years, but it was a troubled relationship, with lots of violence and abuse.

Being later born, I escaped all that directly, of course, but it impacted me indirectly through how my older siblings were affected. Our relationships were influenced by the things they went through—hurts and wounds can be like stones dropped into a pond, causing ripples to flow outward.

CHAPTER 2

Though she was the oldest of all my half-siblings, Cheryl was more like a mom to me in many ways. If I woke up afraid when Mom was out drinking somewhere when I was small, I would go and slip into bed with Cheryl, and she would comfort me.

Cheryl was the first of the five children born to Mom and Tony. While they were kind about my dad, no one in the family I have spoken to ever had a good word to say about Tony. Not only was he lazy, but he was also mean. Among the stories I heard was when my mom was standing on a chair to change a light bulb. Heavily pregnant then, she did or said something that irritated Tony badly. He knocked her off the chair and kicked her in the stomach as she lay on the ground.

Another time, when she was carrying a baby again, they were out in the car when they got into an argument. Tony pulled the vehicle over to the side of the road and pushed her out into a ditch, leaving her in the pouring rain as he drove away. On occasions, he would burn her with cigarettes.

Though I never knew him personally, I experienced some of Tony's legacy through the trickle-down impact he had. His mistreatment wasn't restricted to his wife. His kids also experienced abuse. Cheryl spoke of being beaten by him—she moved out as soon as she could, at sixteen—and I can't help but suspect that some of the problems my brothers Garry and Jack had were related to what they experienced.

Cheryl told me they all suffered at their father's hands, but for some reason, Garry was singled out for special attention. Tony would repeatedly hit him on the head, making me wonder if that contributed to what clearly became some serious mental problems. Some of Tony's apparent dislike for Garry might have had something to do with the fact that he was kind of slow on the uptake. He would get teased about it a lot at school. The kids there would pick on him because he wasn't as bright as they were and because it was clear from the way he dressed that we were poor. One day in eighth grade, Garry was being goaded again when he just lost it. He picked up a desk and started swinging it around at people.

That got him kicked out of school, which seemed to accelerate his decline. By the time he was fourteen or so, he was living on the streets, sometimes finding an unlocked car he could sleep in. He'd cycle back through the house from time to time, but then he would start acting too crazy again, and Mom would kick him out once more. He drifted in and out of work, never able to hold a job down for long.

Garry was around seventeen or eighteen when he was back with us during the summer, taking a nap in the middle of the day. He was woken up by a guy mowing his lawn down the street, and he was very unhappy about it. He went down there and told the man to stop cutting his grass so he could get some sleep. As you might imagine, the guy told Garry he would cut his grass whenever he felt like it—only not as politely as that.

Garry returned to the house and pulled the handle off a broken mower out in the garage. Then he took it back down the street and started clubbing the guy with it. Garry was arrested for attempted murder and sent to prison, where his decline only intensified. I heard he tried to kill himself a couple of times while he was there, once by eating a light bulb.

On his release, Garry drifted between our house, other family members' homes, friends' couches, and the streets. Mom had him admitted to a psychiatric hospital at one stage to see if he could get some help, but nothing came of it. I remember visiting him there, being freaked out by seeing a woman patient smearing feces over herself and thinking how fragile and lost Garry seemed.

Other than one occasion, I never directly experienced Garry's anger. He was kind and gentle toward me, just not quite all there. He often seemed trapped someplace else in his head. At least, that's what I attribute some of his actions to. Like when he decided he wanted some cheese toast, using the new toaster Mom had just gotten with some Green Stamps she had saved up. Garry just dropped a slice of bread and a slice of cheese into the toaster and wondered why it melted everywhere, ruining the new toaster. Mom was furious with him.

His quirky manner and appearance were accentuated by a mishap when he was about twelve. He was having a slingshot war with some friends when one of them fired and caught him right in the mouth. The stone broke one of his two main front teeth in half, giving him a crooked smile to go with his lopsided personality. We didn't have the money for him to get it fixed, and it became just another reason for people to make fun of him.

Because he was self-conscious about how he looked, he never smiled, which only made him seem even moodier than he was.

Over time, Garry's alcohol and drug use got worse. He may have been self-medicating, but using LSD didn't help improve his mental state. Even Mom got exasperated with the way he was living. When she discovered that he was growing pot plants out behind our garage during one of his stays back in the house, she went mad and mowed them all down. That provoked a massive fight between the two of them.

Garry's struggles were exacerbated by his relationship with Jack. Four years younger than Garry, Jack was everything he wasn't and wanted to be—good-looking, outgoing, popular. Jack's blond hair and blue eyes attracted the girls, and his badass manner intimidated the boys, which worked in my favor.

When I was in second grade, some kids at school started teasing me about a speech impediment I had at the time. Then, another boy came over and warned them off. "You know who his big brother is?" he asked them. When they learned I was related to Jack, they backed away, telling me they were really sorry.

If he didn't go looking for trouble, it came for him. Jack was in ninth grade when the authorities decided to integrate the Dallas schools. It was a big change for the Black and White kids who had grown up in mostly separate communities. Jack regularly came home from school bearing the marks of another fight, either one he had initiated or been forced into.

Having a big brother everyone thought was cool bestowed a certain amount of prestige on me. I liked to be associated with him and always accepted when he offered to let me tag along despite my being so much younger. He would take me out in his

Dodge Super Bee 440, a muscle car that turned all heads, boys and girls alike. Jack would gun the engine, telling me that he didn't think he would make it to thirty, just like his hero James Dean, who died at the wheel of his Porsche.

One time, when I was about twelve, we were out riding around and smoking weed when the police pulled us over. Jack slipped the bag of marijuana he had with him under his seat.

The police officer approached Jack's window and asked if we had been smoking grass. Jack told him no.

"Don't lie to me, boys," the officer said. "I can smell it on you."

"Okay, we smoked one joint," Jack said. "We don't have anymore."

The officer sighed. "We could do this the easy way or the hard way," he said. Did we want to be handcuffed at the side of the road where all our friends could see us while he took the vehicle apart, or would we cooperate?

Jack reached down, pulled out the bag of weed, and handed it over.

"Okay," the officer said, "let this be your lesson. I'm going to let you go now. Have a good day."

I breathed a sigh of relief as we drove away, but Jack was ticked. "I'll bet he's gonna smoke that himself," he fumed. "I should call 911 and tell them he stole my weed!"

Though having Jack as my brother offered some protection from others, it didn't keep me safe from him. I knew to be very careful not to provoke his hair-trigger temper. Being closer in age, he and Garry would often get into all-out brawls. Things only got worse when Jack was drinking. He told me a couple of stories that hinted at the dark side of him I saw occasionally. He recounted throwing a beer bottle at a guy who was cycling by one time, knocking the poor man off his bike and pitching him over the side of a bridge and down to the rocks below. Jack and his buddies just laughed.

THOUGH HAVING JACK AS MY BROTHER OFFERED SOME PROTECTION FROM OTHERS, IT DIDN'T KEEP ME SAFE FROM HIM.

Another time, he and some friends got into trouble after breaking into some houses and stealing some property. Then they discovered who had ratted on them to the police. Jack told me how they took the guy to a junkyard by a river not far from where we lived, where they chained him to the hood of a car, beat him, and then threw him into the water. The nonchalant way he spoke about those events made me think he wasn't telling them for effect.

I met my half-sister Rita only once. Born a couple of years before Jack, she was long gone by the time I arrived, and no one ever really spoke about her. There are different stories as to how and why she wasn't in the home, which I have never been able to substantiate. The common thread is that the authorities took away Rita because she was mistreated somehow, but that leaves the question about the other kids being allowed to stay.

I was about sixteen when Cheryl called me one day and said she wanted me to go to her place to meet a sister I didn't know about. It may sound strange to say I took that in my stride, but having grown up in an environment where things changed all the time and you were never quite sure about what you had been told, it simply didn't seem too odd to me that no one had ever mentioned this before. I went over and spent an afternoon with Rita, a pretty and pleasant blond teenager. The fact that we were related somehow didn't really register or have any deep meaning.

This wasn't the only surprise I had around that time. Reminiscing with Mom about one of the houses we had lived in longer than any other, I asked her what had happened to little Ricky? The cutest little guy, with dark hair, kind of like mine, had lived next door with his single mom, an older woman. Though he was a couple of years younger than me, I had always enjoyed playing with him and keeping an eye out for him. Many times, I'd push him in the swing set in his yard.

"Oh yes," Mom said, "I've been meaning to tell you about that. He was your brother."

Remarkably, I took this revelation in my stride; it was just another piece of the crazy puzzle of my life. Mom went on to remind me about the time she'd been pregnant and gone to the hospital, only to return alone and tell us the baby had died during delivery. Well, he hadn't, she said. But she had been so overwhelmed with caring for the children she already had that she didn't think she could cope with another, so she gave him to our neighbor.

Rather than feeling mad at Mom, I felt sorry for her. As she told me what had happened, she said that one of the agreements between her and the neighbor had been that my mom was never to let on to Ricky about their relationship. Mom said there were times when she would go out into the backyard and look over to see Ricky playing outside, and she would weep because she couldn't go over and hug him.

RATHER THAN FEELING MAD AT MOM, I FELT SORRY FOR HER.

Then there was Betty. I learned about her during this same span of two or three years in which I heard of Rita and Ricky, on the way to a family gathering. "I just want you to know there's a sister I've never told you about, and she's looking forward to meeting you," Mom said casually. Betty had been born after Jack, she said. "I was in a bad way, so I gave her to Uncle Billy [her father's brother] to raise."

At the reunion, my previously unknown half-sister came over to speak with me. She was pretty and kind. We chatted about this and that for an hour or so before she got up to leave. "I wish we'd known each other growing up," she told me.

Those revelations go some way toward explaining how I wasn't too fazed when I learned about Jeffrey all those years later.

Only once I was out of that kind of topsy-turvy world could I begin to see how upside-down things were and how fortunate

I was to have escaped some of the struggles some of my siblings had. While I managed to find a straight new path, their wanderings continued.

The last time I saw Garry was on a visit to Mom's in Canton, Texas, where she had moved back after a time living in Louisiana. He was staying with her when my wife, Kim, and I took our firstborn down to meet their grandmother from our home in Wyoming. I couldn't help but feel sorry for him, living on disability, with no prospects and no sense of purpose. "You're so lucky you're normal," he told me during one of our conversations. "You have a wife and a kid ... That's never going to happen for me. I'm never going to be normal."

Two weeks later, I was on a shift in the produce section of the grocery store where I worked when I got summoned to the phone. In the days before cell phones, getting a call like this meant some kind of major event had just taken place. Mom was on the line, screaming and crying. "I killed your brother!" she wailed. "I killed your brother!" I couldn't make sense of what she was saying; had there been some kind of an accident? "Sometimes you kill people with words," she said obscurely. Finally, she calmed down enough to tell me more. She and Garry had clashed that morning, she said. She had told him that he was worthless, that he was a burden she was always going to have to carry. A little later, she had gone out into the garage and found his body hanging there.

For a season, Jack seemed to have escaped the family's demons. After another run-in with the law, he was given an ultimatum in court: join the military or go to jail. Jack chose the army and did well for himself. He got a job as a prison guard and told me once, "Jackie, it's like a family reunion here: I've seen cousins I haven't seen in years."

Then things began to unravel. He started drinking more and lost his job after a domestic incident involving his wife. By the time he came to visit Kim, our five kids, and me, he was in a bad way. He told stories about being pursued by hitmen, and how he had an evil twin who was going around committing crimes that he was getting in trouble for. I didn't know where fact and fantasy parted ways, but I knew I couldn't risk having him around my family, so I reluctantly asked him to leave.

In 2015, Jack was arrested for triple homicide. A feud with people across the street from where he lived in Dallas flared up for some reason, and he went over there with a shotgun, barged in, and opened fire on four people. Only one survived.

Writing to me from the mental institution to which he was sent, it became clear Jack's mind had derailed somewhere. In rambling letters, he recalled bizarre episodes from the past that had never happened. He told me how he'd been a stuntman in the movie *Butch Cassidy and the Sundance Kid*, and that the volleyball Tom Hanks had talked with in that famous scene from *Castaway* had been his—the weirdest stuff. One time, he called our home while I was away for work, telling Kim that I had been kidnapped.

Sad as I was, I realized that there was nothing I could do for Jack other than pray for him. Over time, the letters stopped arriving.

Given how I learned about my family in dribs and drabs, I'm reconciled to the fact that there may yet be other siblings somewhere that I don't know about. In fact, I learned of two while writing this book. Researching my father, I found records of a marriage before he met Mom, which produced two children, both of whom are deceased. There was also some family chatter about Dad fathering another child by someone else while he and Mom were together, though I have never been able to get to the bottom of that.

How does it feel to learn of close blood relatives you never knew about and will never have the chance to meet—at least, this side of heaven? Strangely, not much.

CHAPTER 3

Mom prided herself on the fact that while we might be white trash, we weren't trailer park trash, whom she considered to be the lowest of the low. I knew some kids from school who lived in trailer parks, and their homes were nicer than our rented house, and they seemed to have more money than we did, but I didn't debate the issue with her.

For some reason, it also mattered to Mom that we always lived in a house, not an apartment. Somehow, that seemed to provide a higher status for her. And with what seemed like an endlessly revolving list of family members passing through our place—not only the older siblings who would come and go but other relatives from time to time—it offered a little more space.

The accommodation was still squeezed, though. Tracy, my younger sister, and I often shared a room. When some of our older siblings were back for a while, we might have to give up our beds for a pallet on the floor and a blanket. There wasn't a lot of furniture, and what we did have either came secondhand or from the surrounding streets in Pleasant Grove, in southeast Dallas, one of the city's poorer communities. We'd go out on "hard trash night" to see what other people had discarded that we could use. I'd try to overlook the stains on the used mattresses.

Cramped quarters meant you learned more than you might want to know about and from other people. When I was about eight or nine, Jack and I shared a bunk bed for a while. As a teenager who had discovered girls, he would sometimes bring his latest girlfriend back to his—our—room. He would throw a blanket over his lower bunk so I couldn't see what was going on, but I could tell from the sounds that they were having sex. I'd lie there feeling kind of gross and irritated.

When Mom was between marriages, I had mixed feelings when she'd go out to the bar regularly—four or five nights a week—not knowing whether she'd come back with some random guy she had met. Part of me liked the security of knowing a man was in the house; it gave me a sense of safety. But part of me also hated the reason they were there. In a small house, it was pretty evident what was going on. I'd lay there with a pillow over my head. In one place we lived in, the bedrooms had no doors for some reason. Mom hung a red curtain over the entrance to her room. One night, I woke up with a bad dream, stumbled into her room, and quickly backed out. I never mentioned to her what I had seen.

I did what I could to shield Tracy from what was going on. She was too young to really understand, but I didn't want her even to have questions. If I heard her stirring in the night, I would go over and lay down next to her and tell her a story to distract her until she went back to sleep.

Tracy and I would run out to the mailbox excitedly every day as the end of the month neared, with our mouths watering. We were looking for that distinctive envelope we knew arrived then, the one with the food stamps in it. Mom's monthly $167 welfare check had run out by that stage, and the $65 of food stamps was like the cavalry arriving. If they were there, it was going to be a good day and a good following week.

First, we'd maybe each get a dollar stamp from Mom to spend just as we wanted at the corner store. I'd choose the barbecue sandwich, a Coke, and a bag of chips. Tracy always went for a Totino's frozen pizza, a packet of pink Hostess snowballs, and a red strawberry soda. Her choice was torture for me because I'd have to wait to eat until we got home, and she had heated her pizza in the oven. It took some time, and every second seemed like an eternity. Then, finally, it was ready, and we'd sit there dining like we were royalty.

> THE $65 OF FOOD STAMPS WAS LIKE THE CAVALRY ARRIVING. IF THEY WERE THERE, IT WAS GOING TO BE A GOOD DAY AND A GOOD FOLLOWING WEEK.

With that food sitting satisfyingly in our stomachs, we'd head off to the grocery store with Mom. We didn't exactly go crazy, but we certainly ate better for a while. In fact, we often wouldn't eat at all the last few days of the month because we had no money: we were into intermittent fasting before it became a thing, by necessity, not design.

With the food stamps, we'd get real milk, cereal (generic, not brand names, because they were pricier), and a pound of bologna and some bread. It wasn't gourmet, but the occasional fried hamburger patty or hot sausage links were delicious, given our usual basic menus.

Giving her some due, Mom was quite creative with the limited resources she had to hand. One of my favorite special meals was her tomato gravy and biscuits. Another treat was beanie weenies, baked beans with hot dogs on top, baked in the oven. If one of us went fishing and caught some crappie or perch, we could look forward to them being rolled in cornmeal and fried with potatoes. To this day, the thought of any of these simple meals makes my mouth water. Maybe when you're used to the same old, same old, anything different seems really exotic.

Once the food stamp purchases had run out, we defaulted to a more basic diet again. Lots of pinto beans—the smell would hit you when you came in through the door—sometimes with a piece of cornbread to mix things up. Mom did her best to provide some variety. There might be bean patties for breakfast—more pinto beans, fried with a powdered egg and some flour. Sometimes, there'd be grits as an alternative.

Depending on how tight the money was, Tracy and I would get signed up for free meals at school, which I always enjoyed. Sausage and eggs for breakfast! Plus, you got an afternoon snack of cookies and milk. However, I was a little self-conscious about handing over the school lunch program tickets to get my meal in the cafeteria. The bright orange voucher clearly showed everyone that you were on welfare. I'd get my food and then hover near the register, waiting until no one was around to pass the kitchen staff my ticket. It didn't occur to me that many of my friends were probably part of the free food program, too.

Being hungry was commonplace. Some nights, we'd go to bed without having had anything to eat for supper. If I complained to Mom, she'd say, "But didn't you have lunch at school?" I got used to the quiet gnawing sensation in my stomach.

I'm not proud of this, but I made a point of befriending a kid who lived down the street. I didn't really like him at all; in fact, he was pretty obnoxious. Eat-your-own-boogers-level obnoxious. But his fridge was always full of food. Packets of Butterball lunch meat which, put between two slices of white bread with some mac and cheese and microwaved, made the most amazing sandwich. Even more remarkable was that they had name-brand cereals in the cupboard, like Cap'n Crunch and Fruit Loops. I couldn't believe how wealthy his family must be.

> BEING HUNGRY WAS COMMONPLACE. SOME NIGHTS, WE'D GO TO BED WITHOUT HAVING HAD ANYTHING TO EAT FOR SUPPER.

Mom never had a job because she didn't want to lose her welfare benefits. Once a month, we'd get a visit from a social worker, checking to see that we still qualified for government assistance. If we'd gotten anything that might be considered "extra" since the last time because of some of her side dealings, Mom would hide it away in a closet. If we were fortunate enough to have a television set for the time being—they came and went as the money fluctuated, along with a phone—she would throw a blanket over it, as if no one would know what was underneath.

While she chose not to get a regular job, Mom had an entrepreneurial side I'm sure she could have developed if she had put her mind to it. One way she'd supplement our meager income was by taking us out junking on a Saturday. Tracy and I would pile into the car with her, and we would head out into the countryside on the outskirts of Dallas, looking for abandoned properties. We'd pretend not to see any of the "Keep Out" signs on the fences. Having checked there was no one around, we'd go inside to see what we might find. Sometimes, these places were unlocked, so it seemed like we weren't really trespassing, just visiting, but then we'd come across one when the doors were bolted. Mom would then look for an open window to boost me in through so I could climb inside and open the door from the other side.

Part of me knew what we were doing wasn't quite right, but any time I could get to spend with Mom when she wasn't at the bar was a good day, so I rationalized to my young self that we weren't really doing anything wrong. Plus, there was a little buzz of excitement about what we might find. Mom would tell us to look out for rare coins that could be worth a fortune. We never found anything like that, but on one "visit," I discovered a Hot Wheels set and a metal toy car from the television series

Ironside. I thought I'd hit the jackpot, taking them home and playing with them for a long time.

Another time, we got into a house and found an old chest, like something that might have treasure locked away in it. Mom was excited until we opened it to find a pile of old letters, some of them dating back to World War Two, correspondence between a husband in the military and his wife. Mom was disappointed, but as a history buff, I was thrilled; it was like a peek into the living past as I read some of the letters.

You never knew what you were going to find inside those abandoned places. Sometimes, others had been there before us and trashed them. Other times, we were the first ones there, finding items to keep for ourselves and others that Mom could sell in a yard sale.

At one location, a funky smell emanated from the place when we pushed open the door. The source became evident as we explored—there were the bodies of four large dogs, each in a different stage of decomposition. The scent of decay seemed to cling to my skin, and I couldn't shake what I had seen for some time. I kept wondering, how could anyone have left those poor animals in there to die like that? Did no one pass by and hear them barking?

I didn't tell Mom what I was thinking because I didn't want to open up a can of worms there. We had several dogs during my childhood, mutts we would be given by someone else. Tracy and I loved having them; they were something to play with and gave us a sense of protection when Mom was out at night and we were left alone. We could never afford to care for them well—they ate the scraps we didn't want, and they never got taken to a veterinarian. Tracy and I would have to spend hours picking ticks off them.

Then, there'd come a time when Mom decided we couldn't afford even the little amount of money it was costing us to have the dog around. She would insist we climb into the car with her when she drove out into the countryside to open the door and leave the animal standing at the side of the road. I begged her not to do it, saying that I couldn't face the idea of our dog being left out there on its own. "Oh, don't worry," she'd say, "someone will find it and adopt it." I wasn't so sure.

When we shooed the confused dog out of the vehicle, closed the door, and turned around, Mom would tell us not to look back as she drove away. I'd always steal a glance, though, looking to see the creature standing there and seeming to wonder, *What's going on?* For me, it was just another disappointment that got stuffed away inside, another evidence that nothing in this world was permanent, so don't get too attached to anything.

CHAPTER 4

Though we didn't always have a television, it was an important part of our home when it was there. Some of my sweetest memories of Mom are the evenings we'd snuggle up on the sofa to watch her favorite shows, *The Dean Martin Celebrity Roast*[5] and *The Carol Burnett Show*.[6] During the summer, when I didn't have to be up for school in the morning, I'd be allowed to stay up late for *The Tonight Show Starring Johnny Carson*,[7] which was a great treat.

TV evenings were memorable for a couple of reasons. I enjoyed the programs, but more importantly, it meant that Mom was going to stay home with us rather than go out to the bar and leave Tracy and me alone. On weeknights, she would sometimes choose to watch something with us, but there was no way she would stay in on a Saturday night, no matter how much we begged.

If the phone rang, we hoped it wasn't her best friend (another Evelyn) calling because we knew she would ask Mom to go out drinking. When we pleaded with Mom to stay home, she would make it seem like it was our fault she wanted to go out, as though

---

5 *The Dean Martin Celebrity Roast*, Greg Garrison (October 31, 1974; Las Vegas, NV: NBC), Television.
6 *The Carol Burnett Show*, Dave Powers and Clark Jones (September 11, 1967; Los Angeles: CA), Television.
7 *The Tonight Show Starring Johnny Carson*, Frederick Timmins de Cordova (September 27, 1954; New York, NY: NBC Productions), Television.

it was because we were such hard work to care for, and she had to go and get some relief.

When she did go out, the television gave Tracy and me something to do other than play outside, if it was light, or play cards. We didn't have much else in the house to amuse ourselves with. Having a show playing also made us feel safer, as though someone else was in the house with us.

One evening, when I was eight or so, Tracy and I were sitting together watching something when we suddenly saw a face at the window staring in at us. I was scared; I'd overheard someone tell Mom a few days earlier that there was a peeping tom in the neighborhood. I ran to the phone—thankfully, we had one at the time—and called where I knew Mom might be.

> **HAVING A SHOW PLAYING ALSO MADE US FEEL SAFER, AS THOUGH SOMEONE ELSE WAS IN THE HOUSE WITH US.**

It would be one of two places: Fat Albert's, just down the street, or the Debonair Club, a little farther away. I could picture Fat Albert's in my mind because Mom had taken Tracy and me there a couple of times when she went during the day. She had us play shuffleboard in the corner while she sat at the bar. I remember the low lights, the smell of cigarette smoke, and a pallor of fear and sadness hanging over the place.

When Mom came to the phone, I told her what had happened with the guy at the window. I said we were really scared and asked what I should do.

"I've told you not to call me when I'm at the bar," she said. "Go figure it out." Then she hung up. I made sure all the doors were locked and held Tracy tight as we sat on the sofa. Finally, exhausted, we took ourselves off to bed.

The following day, I went outside to investigate; our window was too high for the guy to have been able to look in on us without some leg-up. Sure enough, an old desk we had moved outside had been dragged from where we had put it at the side of the house to under the window. I showed Mom to prove to her I hadn't been making things up.

She was dismissive. "A lot of people have talked about him," she said. "He's not going to hurt you. If he'd wanted to, he'd have done that by now."

Another evening when we were alone, there was a knock at the door. I answered, and there was a guy there who said he was from the rental center and had come to collect the TV because we'd made no payment for a couple of months. Tracy and I started crying, begging him not to take it away, but he ignored us and left with the set.

Though it wasn't unusual for Tracy and me to be left to fend for ourselves, typically we knew Mom would be back sometime before morning. Then there was the weekend she went on a girls' trip to Galveston when I was about eight. She told us that she had tried to arrange for someone to come over and watch us while she was gone but that the plans had fallen through. "So, you can just stay in the house by yourselves, okay?" she said as she left, Tracy tearfully begging her to stay.

Mom left us on Friday afternoon with a single piece of bologna in the fridge. Tracy and I didn't eat that evening because we'd had lunch at school that day, and I knew we needed to stretch what was available. On Saturday, I cut the slice in half and fried it because it tasted better that way. We had the remaining piece on Sunday before Mom breezed in from her weekend jaunt as if she'd just been down to the store for an hour.

Having a television didn't just fill my time. In some ways, it filled my heart. I saw something in shows like *The Brady Bunch*,[8] *The Waltons*,[9] and *Little House on the Prairie*[10] that held out a promise of more. The stories often had some kind of teaching moment about doing the right thing and being kind. I felt a pang of envy watching families who loved each other, cared for each other, and had each other's backs. And I wished that Mike Brady, John Walton, or Charles Ingalls were my father. I admired these surrogate dads' strong character, their sense of duty, and their belief in right and wrong. I knew I wanted to grow up and be just like them one day.

One *Little House on the Prairie*[11] episode made a particular impression on me. "The Lord is My Shepherd" was a two-part story in which the Ingalls' daughter, Laura, ran away from home because she felt guilty for not praying for her sickly newborn brother. Up in the mountains, she was befriended by Jonathan,

---
[8] *The Brady Bunch*, Oscar Rudolf et. al. (September 26, 1969; Burbank, CA: ABC Studios), Television.
[9] *The Waltons*, Harry Harris et. al. (September 14, 1972; Los Angeles, CA: CBS Studios), Television.
[10] *Little House on the Prairie*, William F. Claxton et. al. (September 11, 1974; Manhattan, NY: NBC Productions), Television.
[11] *Little House on the Prairie*, NBC, Television.

a kind man (played by Ernest Borgnine) who watched over her until her father came and found her.

> **I ADMIRED THESE SURROGATE DADS' STRONG CHARACTER, THEIR SENSE OF DUTY, AND THEIR BELIEF IN RIGHT AND WRONG. I KNEW I WANTED TO GROW UP AND BE JUST LIKE THEM ONE DAY.**

Mom wasn't impressed by these shows, however. Whenever she caught me watching one of them, she would say something negative. Like, that was all just a fairy tale—there were no good men like that out there, there were no stable families like that. They all probably had skeletons in their closet.

In the absence of television, I loved to read. Two books in particular enthralled me: Maurice Sendak's *Where the Wild Things Are*[12] and Robb White's *Deathwatch*.[13] In hindsight, it's not hard to see the appeal. Sendak's illustrated children's book featured a boy sent to bed without his supper who stood up to monsters. White's young adult novel recounted a young man's fight to survive after being abandoned in the wilderness. I read

---
12 Maurice Sendak, *Where the Wild Things Are* (New York, NY: HarperCollins, 1984).
13 Robb Shite, *Deathwatch* (New York, NY: Laurel Leaf, 1983).

and re-read both books. The *Richie Rich*[14] comic books were a favorite, too; I imagined what it must be like to live like he did, never wanting for anything.

I also loved watching sports whenever we did have a television. I was a huge Dallas Cowboys fan and idolized their quarterback, Roger Staubach. "Captain Comeback," as he was known, epitomized manliness for me. Strong, dependable, honest—pretty much the opposite of most of the men circulating in my life. I pretended that he was my dad. I'd go out in the backyard and throw a ball around by myself, imagining we were tossing it to each other.

More than anything, I longed to have a Dallas Cowboys uniform, but we didn't have the money. Then, one Christmastime, I got a uniform with Staubach's name on the back in a gift program through The Salvation Army, which helped needy families. I was over the moon and wore that thing until I could no longer squeeze into it.

The Salvation Army rescued more than one Christmas for us, but there were several when we didn't get anything. Before I discovered the truth about Santa Claus, I decided he mustn't like me for some reason. I'd go to the mall, sit on his lap, and tell him what I wanted, only to be disappointed. There was the time I asked for a BB gun: nothing. More than one year, I asked for a football; again, nothing.

One Christmas, I compared notes with a kid in the neighborhood I'd play with sometimes. We both had a football on the top of our wish list, but neither of us got one on Christmas morning.

---

14 Alfred Harvey and Warren Kremer, *The Richie Rich Comic Series* (New York, NY: Harvey Comics, 1953).

After commiserating with each other for a while, we got hold of some aluminum foil and rolled it into a football shape to play with out in the street. Another Christmastime, I begged and begged Mom for us to at least have a tree. She said no, we couldn't afford it, so I took a butcher's knife from the kitchen and went out into the fields near where we lived. I found a small pine tree and cut it down. It took several hours, but eventually, I was able to drag it home, so we had a tree for the holidays.

If there was one person in our extended family who was something of a safe harbor in all the stormy seas, it was Aunt Alice, my mom's baby sister.

She, her husband, and their three children lived not too far away from us, and we would spend time with them all—when Mom wasn't on the outs with them. I spent more time with Lena, Bubba, and Sheri than any of my other cousins.

Though Mom and Aunt Alice were close, they had a mercurial relationship, just like Mom seemed to have with everyone, and sometimes there would be long periods when they did not speak. "You're not a real member of the family until Evelyn has gone off on you and thrown you out of the house," Aunt Alice told me recently with a chuckle.

The getting-thrown-out part wasn't an exaggeration. Once, Aunt Alice and her daughter, Sheri, went down to visit Mom for the weekend, and there was some kind of a falling out. Mom got so upset that she said they needed to leave, even though it was late at night. When Aunt Alice and Sheri got to their car, it had a flat tire. There was no spare, so they had to wait until the morning to have someone come and fix it so they could leave, but Mom wouldn't have them back in the house. They had to spend the night in the car.

I experienced the same kind of thing early in my marriage. I went down to Texas, where Mom and her current husband, Royce, were living at the time, with Kim, the two kids we had at the time, and Kim's parents. It was to be a bring-the-families-together time. The first couple of days went well, all of us squeezed into their trailer. But then it went south. Mom freaked out over something and told us we were no longer welcome. We piled into our cars and went and spent the night with Cheryl before returning home to Wyoming.

Like us, Aunt Alice didn't have much money, but she was always very welcoming and caring when we visited. Cheryl lived with them for a period when she wanted to get away from our home. Sadly, all three of Aunt Alice's children have passed, but I remember Bubba with special affection for something he did. He and his sisters were staying with us for a few days, one time, and he saw that my shoes were in really bad condition, worn and holey. Unless we had absolutely grown out of them, we only ever got one pair a year and had to make do. Bubba and I were about the same size, so he let me wear his newer shoes to school so the other kids wouldn't make fun of me and my ratty pair. His was a pair of stylish black-and-white Converse, and I was so happy to wear them that I was sad when he and his sisters went home. When the kids at school wanted to know what had happened to my new shoes the next week, I told a story about them having been stolen.

Bubba may have gotten that sensitivity from his mom. She noticed things in a way that made you feel special. I liked to wear cologne from being a young teenager, and Aunt Alice would always compliment me on it and say how good I smelled. She didn't have much money, but from time to time, she'd buy me a nice scent and give it to me on the condition I promised to wear it when she was around.

She also spoke some rare words of encouragement to me. When John Anderson's "I'm Just an Old Chunk of Coal (But I'm Going to Be a Diamond Someday)"[15] came on the radio when I was around seventeen, Aunt Alice made a point of telling me that it made her think of me. She reminded me of that during a recent visit. "And you did become a diamond, Jackie, didn't you?" she said, making me feel proud. Today, I use that song as my walk-up music when I'm going on-stage to speak at conferences.

---

15 Billy Joe Shaver, vocalist, "I'm Just an Old Chunk of Coal (But I'm Gonna Be a Diamond Someday)" by Billy Joe Shaver, released March 28, 1981, track 5 on *John Anderson 2*, Warner Bros. Nashville.

CHAPTER 5

School was something of an oasis for me, a still center in all the chaos. Though we moved houses a lot, it was always within the same general area, so I attended the same school until sixth grade when the city of Dallas decided to integrate schools and started busing us across town.

While most kids couldn't wait for school to be over, I loved being there. It was safe, there was food, and there were people who showed an interest in me. Until I got more focused on girls and partying as a teenager, I was a diligent student, and though the teachers would sometimes have to rein in my sociable tendencies, I wasn't deliberately disruptive. Progress reports often commented on my need to be less of a chatterbox.

> **WHILE MOST KIDS COULDN'T WAIT FOR SCHOOL TO BE OVER, I LOVED BEING THERE. IT WAS SAFE, THERE WAS FOOD, AND THERE WERE PEOPLE WHO SHOWED AN INTEREST IN ME.**

There were probably a couple of reasons for my talkativeness. Growing up in an environment with always some kind of potential threat meant I had my internal radar running all the time. That made me ultra-aware of what was happening around me, so I was constantly distracted by things and wanted to point them out to others.

Plus, I was making up for some lost time. Up until I was in third grade, I had a quite severe speech impediment. I couldn't pronounce words clearly, though that didn't stop me from running my mouth a mile a minute. But it did mean that, outside of the home, people didn't understand what I was going on about, so in some ways that limited the interaction we could have. At home, Mom and Cheryl, particularly among my siblings, learned to decipher what my mumbles meant, or I just pointed at things until I got what I needed. Mom explained away my difficulty by saying that it was because I was spoiled, so I didn't need to learn to speak clearly because people were always willing to help me out.

Strangely enough, I wasn't embarrassed by my inability to be understood. There was a little bit of teasing at school—one time, I came home and told Mom that one of the kids had called me a "motherfutter," and she just cracked up. But there was never so much made of my problem by other kids that I was left feeling self-conscious about it. I just blew it off.

Actually, I was more sensitive about my name. I was always Jackie Wayne at home and didn't mind that because it reminded me of Dad. But at school, I was called Jackie, which I thought sounded too much like a girl's name. Whenever new students came to the school, I'd always make a point of telling them my name was Jackie, like Jackie Cooper from *The Little Rascals*[16] or Jackie Stewart, the racing driver. When I reached my teens, I announced that I was now Jack.

As I got older, it became clear that something needed to be done about my inability to speak clearly; this wasn't a childhood thing I would grow out of. I got placed with a speech therapist at school for a one-on-one class every day. As far as I know, no one ever delved into whether my speech problem had anything to do with my home environment.

Only once did anyone at school ever question what was happening at home. It was winter, when the cold was as much of a problem as the heat was in the summertime. Just as we had one fan for cooling, we had one gas heater for warming the house. I was standing too close to it one morning when I brushed my right calf against the clay tiles, leaving a nasty brand mark. It stung something awful, and Mom put some butter on it to soothe it.

The pain got worse as the day went on, and I ended up telling my teacher I was hurting. She took me to the school nurse for help. When she saw the bright weal, the nurse looked concerned. "How did this happen, Jackie?' she asked. "Did someone do this to you, or was it an accident? You can tell me."

I was surprised. It was an accident, I said, explaining how I'd gotten too close to the heater. My teacher and the nurse conferred, and then they called in the principal. She took a look at the wound and asked me the same questions. I gave the same answer, and eventually, they let me return to class. When I told Mom about it later that day, she just shrugged.

---

16 Penelope Spheeris, *The Little Rascals* (August 5, 1994; Universal City: CA, Amblin Entertainment).

The speech specialist assigned to help me was kind and patient and didn't make me feel like I was being singled out because I was stupid. She used a mirror to help me see how to form sounds more clearly with my tongue as I spoke, and by the end of that school year, I was talking as clearly as anyone. I even got a certificate for outstanding achievement in speech therapy.

I remember two of my regular teachers with special affection. When I was in third grade, Miss Berry announced she would be retiring at the end of the year. She seemed ancient, with her gray hair always swept up in a bun and old-fashioned dresses. But she was always kind to me. When the other kids talked about getting her parting gifts, I wanted to as well, only I didn't have any money.

When I told Mom about it, she pulled out a little jewelry box with pieces she had picked up here and there—and who knows where—and told me to choose something. I selected a small cameo locket on a chain. All the kids gave Miss Berry their gifts at a special thank-you gathering a few weeks before the end of the term. When I handed her mine, she gave me a look of delight. My offering wasn't anywhere as lavish as some of the others, but Miss Berry wore my locket every day until she left. I felt so special.

Then, there was Miss Bransfield in fifth grade. She was fresh out of college and super-pretty, with a sweet face set with kind blue eyes. All of that appealed to my awakening hormones, but she was also very enthusiastic and made me want to learn. Being chosen to clean the chalkboard for her felt like a badge of honor.

Not that I was a teacher's pet. The other kids didn't get on to me for sucking up. In fact, I had a bit of a reputation as the class clown, always looking to make everyone laugh. In my second-hand clothes, I knew I wouldn't win any best-dressed awards, so I decided to go for the funny guy prize. When Mom bought me an old black leather jacket from Goodwill, in junior high, I'd wear it with the collar turned up and comb back my hair like Fonzie from *Happy Days*[17] to get a laugh.

Much as I enjoyed school, I didn't get to participate in any extracurricular activities—we just didn't have the money. I was a reasonably decent athlete and would have loved to try out for basketball, baseball, and even football, even though I was pretty scrawny, but Mom said no because it would mean having to buy shoes and uniforms that we couldn't afford.

I did get to join the Cub Scout group that met at the Fireside Recreation Center, not far from where we lived, for a year or so, which I enjoyed. They waived the fee so I could participate. I thought the other boys looked really cool in their uniforms, but we couldn't afford all that. I had to make do with a tee shirt with the Webelos ("We'll Be Loyal Scouts") acronym on it. There were just two of us in the group who dressed like that, making us stand out a bit as the poor kids. While I was part of the group, we were taken to a Baylor-Houston football game in Waco, my first-ever live sporting event, which was great.

Only one thing—or, rather, one person—spoiled my enjoyment of school for a while. When I was in fourth grade, Clifford was the bully we all tried to avoid. He threw his weight around on everybody, and my turn came one day when we were outside playing baseball. He started in on me, making fun of my raggedy

---

[17] *Happy Days*, Garry Marshall (January 15, 1974; Burbank, CA: ABC) Television.

clothes. I ignored him, hoping he would give up when I failed to rise to his bait. And then James Reeves stepped in.

He had come to the school fairly recently, and I knew him a little because we were in the same class, but we weren't really friends. For some reason, James confronted Clifford and knocked him to the ground. Big for his age, he straddled the bully, pinned him, and gave him a couple of pops to the face. "You will never make fun of Jackie again, you got it?" he said.

After that, no one ever had trouble with Clifford again, and James and I became firm friends. We'd hang out together after school at his house, sharing candy he would buy for us from a store we would pass on the walk there. I loved being at his home because there was always plenty of food and things to do.

James had a room of his own, which I thought was the coolest thing, and I'd get to sleep over with him sometimes. Saturday nights were the best because it meant his mom would fix us a big breakfast of eggs, bacon, and toast the following morning. They had a TV that never got repossessed, and James had a minibike we rode around in his backyard.

Another quiet draw to his home was that he had a mom and dad there, unlike most of the other kids I knew, who were in single-parent families or, like me, in ones with a procession of different men. James's mom was sweet and loving. She reminded me a little of Tammy Wynette, whose music she loved to play. She always ensured we had plenty to eat, calling us in from playing outside for snacks and lunch. James's dad was tall and slender and worked at a factory. When he came home, his overalls would always be covered in grease, and he would go and change before coming to the dinner table. He was a little stern but not in an off-putting way. I loved the quiet sense of order that permeated their home.

    James and I remained tight through fourth and fifth grade before we were separated when we went to different junior highs. I didn't see as much of him after that, but I always remembered his intervention and friendship with appreciation.

CHAPTER 6

Whenever we had big family get-togethers, it would be a time to catch up on who was in prison, who was going to prison, and who had just gotten out of prison—updates shared like other people might swap news about graduations and babies. Once, there was a big celebration after someone realized it was the first time no one was locked up right then: everyone showed up in prison orange to mark the occasion. Another time, one of my aunts observed that we had relatives in prison in twelve different states, as though it was some noteworthy record to be celebrated.

As the oldest of the four siblings, Mom's brother, Uncle Sonny, was sort of the unofficial leader of the clan, when he wasn't incarcerated. At the family gatherings, he would sit me on his lap and pass on tips for what to do when I went to prison—when, not if. One piece of advice I remember was drawn from his first time inside at age seventeen. Sitting down at lunch on his first day behind bars, he asked the guys around him who was the biggest, baddest con in the place. Someone pointed out a guy, saying how he had killed his and his wife's families, chopping them up with an ax. "Don't mess with him," Uncle Sonny was warned.

He didn't heed the counsel. Uncle Sonny recalled for me how he picked up his fork and walked over to the man who had been identified to him. "Hey there, I'm Sonny Black," he said. Then he jabbed his fork into the man's cheek as hard as possible.

"Why did you do that?" I asked him incredulously.

"Because everybody saw what I did," he explained. If he was crazy enough to stab the toughest, meanest guy in the place with a fork, nobody was ever going to mess with him, he said. "I just want you to be ready for when you go to prison," he went on. "No matter how much of a badass you're going to be, you're going to get raped in there. And if you don't want that to happen, this is what you have got to do."

But what about the guards, I wanted to know; wouldn't they stop that kind of thing from happening? "They're not gonna help you," he said. "They're either gonna just watch or participate." If I wasn't going to make a statement in the way he had, then I needed to choose one guy to provide sexual favors for, Uncle Sonny went on. "He'll protect you; one guy is better than twenty," he said.

Uncle Sonny's blunt approach to life extended to how he treated women. A good-looking guy with thick black hair and a beard, a little like Kenny Rogers, he always had a woman in tow when he was out of prison. And invariably, she would have some sort of facial bruising. "You know what you tell a woman with two black eyes?" he'd ask me with a grin. "Nothing—you've already told her twice already."

Violence seemed to come as naturally as breathing to him. He told me once how he'd cut the breast of a girlfriend he'd found had been cheating on him. Others in the family recounted equally ugly, and uglier, tales. Uncle Ace told me of when he and Uncle Sonny got into a fight when they were kids. Uncle Sonny drove a pitchfork so deep into Uncle Ace's thigh it came out the other side. On another occasion, Jack recalled an episode he said had transpired when he was out with Uncle Sonny one night. They had been in a bar when Uncle Sonny got into some kind of an argument with another guy. Uncle Sonny said they should take things outside, and as soon as they were out in the alley, he pulled a gun and shot the guy in the stomach. "Let's get the hell out of here," he shouted at Jack, and the two of them hightailed it, not waiting to see how badly injured the guy was.

At family functions, Uncle Sonny always had a silver metal cup in his hand from which he would sip regularly. I must have been around seven or eight when I asked him what was in there.

"Here, see for yourself," he said, handing me his cup.

I took a swig and almost choked on what to me tasted like sour water. Uncle Sonny's drink of choice was pure vodka.

Sometimes, he would slip me a crisp twenty-dollar bill like it was a quarter tossed my way for some candy. That was an unheard-of amount of money, and I asked Mom once where Uncle Sonny got that kind of cash from.

"Oh, he's a consultant," she told me vaguely.

I learned the truth one day when Mom and I went to the post office on Bruton Road, not far from where we lived, so she could get a stamp to mail a letter. There was quite a line, so I looked around to pass the time. My eye caught a photograph on the wall, listing the FBI's current Ten Most Wanted. There was someone I knew staring down at me.

"Mom," I exclaimed as she turned from the counter. "Look, that's Uncle Sonny!"

"Don't be silly," she said, grabbing me by the arm and ushering me out of the post office as people looked at us. "It just looks like him, that's all."

Many years later, she would admit that had, indeed, been Uncle Sonny, wanted for a string of bank robberies all over East Texas. I also learned about the time Garry and Jack had been at a sleepover at someone in the family's house when I was still small. A bunch of the kids had been stretched out, sleeping on the floor the following day, when the front door was kicked in, and there was a posse of FBI agents, shotguns at the ready. They were looking for Uncle Sonny, who had left just the previous day.

Blood may be thicker than water, but when it's mixed with alcohol, relationships can go weird very quickly. Our family was simultaneously bound by a strange sort of loyalty and divided by deep distrust. They would do anything for you when they were sober, which was rare. They would do anything to you when they weren't.

If Mom told me that we were all going to get together for, say, Easter, my stomach would tighten. My cousins and I would band together and try to fade into the corners so the adults didn't notice us. Or we'd say we wanted to go down to the nearby park to play, anything to get out of the way before the alcohol went down and the fists came up.

On more than one occasion, a group of us kids would be playing down the street a ways from whatever house the party was in, and we'd hear the sirens approaching. Things had gotten out of control again, and one of the neighbors had called the police. Next thing we knew, some of the adults would be running past us to get away because they were out on parole and couldn't afford to get caught up in anything. We kids would shrug at each other as if to say, *Family; whatya gonna do?*

> **BLOOD MAY BE THICKER THAN WATER, BUT WHEN IT'S MIXED WITH ALCOHOL, RELATIONSHIPS CAN GO WEIRD VERY QUICKLY.**

I recall one occasion when a poker game was going on, and everybody seemed to be having a good time. We were always only a moment away from mayhem, though, and someone got pissed about something and threw a spoonful of peanut butter at someone else. Had it been a peanut that bounced off harmlessly, it may have passed without incident. But the sticky stuff smeared someone's clothes. That sparked a food fight, which started kind of lighthearted but soon erupted into an all-out brawl with chairs and tables flying and fists swinging. And then the cops arrived again. I sometimes wonder whether the neighbors had 911 on speed dial.

One thing I knew for sure was that I didn't want to get caught up in that kind of craziness when I grew up. And though the adults would talk about law enforcement as if the police were the bad guys, I didn't buy into that idea. It seemed pretty clear to me which side wore the black hats.

The bluster that Uncle Sonny and others displayed when talking about crime and prison didn't impress me. In fact, when I got taken along to visit Uncle Sonny when he was serving time, I realized what a sad figure he was. He tried to act like he was the king of the hill, but in reality, he couldn't cope with life outside an institution.

I'm not sure why Mom dragged me along when she went to visit her brother occasionally. Everything about prison scared me, from the sullen guards cradling their guns in the towers to the way the other prisoners would hoot and holler when you walked through the hallway to the visiting area. "How are you doing, little shithead?" Uncle Sonny would greet me. I was always relieved when it was time to leave.

Given the casual way crime was accepted in the family, the acorns didn't always fall far from the tree. Two of my cousins, William, Uncle Ace's son, and Bobby Joe, Uncle Sonny's boy, were only a couple of years apart and paired up to make some easy money by burglarizing homes.

One evening, they came round to our house and told Mom they'd broken into a bunch of places and had some great stuff if she wanted any of it. We went outside and looked in the trunk, crammed with snow skis and other fancy things. An antique clock caught her eye. She gave them a few bucks for it and sold it sometime later for $150 or so.

> **GIVEN THE CASUAL WAY CRIME WAS ACCEPTED IN THE FAMILY, THE ACORNS DIDN'T ALWAYS FALL FAR FROM THE TREE.**

A WHOLE LIFE

Ten years or so older than I was, William and Bobby Joe were intriguing figures to me, but at the same time, I somehow knew that something wasn't quite right about the way they were living, running fast and loose. Not long after they came round to fence some of their burglary hauls, they literally ran out of road. The two of them were in a car, William at the wheel, as far as anyone knows, when they were in a terrible wreck. The exact details of what happened and why are unclear, but Bobby Joe died.

Though crime was just a way of life in the family, I never felt good about it. Some of those lessons about honesty and fairness from TV shows like *Little House on the Prairie*[18] and *The Waltons*[19] must have lodged deep inside somewhere. The only times I got involved in wrongdoing as a kid was when I had no choice.

I was six or so when we were riding in a car with one of Mom's friends. We passed a house in a nice neighborhood that had two striking lawn jockeys out front, one on either side of the porch. "Hey, I've always wanted one of those," Mom said, signaling her friend to pull over. Then she told me to jump out, grab one of them, and bring it back to the vehicle.

"But Mom...," I began.

"Just do it, Jackie Wayne," she insisted. "They've got two. They don't need both of them."

Everything in me screamed that this was wrong, but I felt I couldn't disobey. Heart pounding, I opened the door, got out, and raced over to the front of the house. Grabbing one of the lawn jockeys, I ran back to the car as fast as possible, and we sped away.

---

18 *Little House on the Prairie*, NBC, Television.
19 *The Waltons*, CBS, Television.

Mom also loved reading the Sunday newspaper, as well as looking through all the coupons, but we couldn't afford to have it delivered. So, she would get me up while it was still dark each Sunday and make me go down the street and bring back a copy of the paper from the front lawn of one of the houses.

What made it even worse for me was that this was where one of my friends lived. One day, I was over there playing with my pal, and I was invited to stay for lunch. While we were eating, my friend's father grumbled about how his Sunday paper had been missing for the last few weeks. "If I catch the son of a bitch that's doing it, I'm going to get my shotgun out, and I'm going to shoot him," he said. I must have gone pale when he said that, but either he didn't notice, or he didn't connect my reaction to guilt.

That was enough for me, though. I was more afraid of getting shot than of disappointing my mother, so I went home and told her I was never doing that again.

Mom's nonchalance about this kind of thing was just the water we swam in at home. On the rare occasions she and Billy, whom she had married when I was a toddler, took us to the movies, she would have Tracy and me lie down in the back of the truck and cover us with a blanket so they didn't have to pay our admission. She would send Garry and Jack out on night-time excursions equipped with an empty plastic milk jug and a length of hose.

Most people left their cars out on their driveway or in the street because they didn't have garages, so the boys would sneak up and siphon gas out of the tanks for our vehicle: this was back before cars had locking gas caps. You had to be careful when you sucked, or you could end up with a mouthful of gasoline. I was dragged along a few times to act as a lookout. On one occasion, Garry and Jack were mid-theft when a light went on in the house. A guy charged out, shouting, "I'm gonna get my gun." We took off running.

CHAPTER 7

Some kids suffer unspeakable abuse; adults use them in ways that can scar their hearts and sear their souls such that only a miracle can heal. I see evidence of that in the lives of some of my siblings and other relatives. They carry into adulthood the unresolved, unreleased pain of being used for sexual gratification by those they should have been able to trust.

Having grown up in a fairly chaotic environment, where appropriate boundaries were not always maintained, and there was a succession of men passing through our home, some of whose backgrounds were sketchy, to say the least, it's remarkable that I somehow emerged largely unscathed. To this day, I don't understand why and how I came through so safely while others did not. I believe part of the answer is that somehow God had His eye and hand on me, though I have no good reason why others were seemingly not as fortunate as me. I believe that, one day, I will meet the guardian angels that God tasked with watching over me, and they will say, "Jack, you sure kept us busy, you know!"

One of the shadowy seasons in which I was somehow sheltered was when Mom was married to Billy. They met on his first day out of prison, which should have been an ample enough warning light for anyone. But Mom was taken in by his good looks and charming manner. All was not good beneath the surface, however. Not only did he never seem to have a steady job, but there was also a dark side to him that led to one of my older sisters moving out of the house and living with one of our aunts. Billy would have his friends over, playing poker until three and four o'clock in the morning.

Billy's wandering eye ended his and Mom's relationship after only a few years—just long enough for Tracy to be born. The last time I saw him, he was leaving the house to walk down to the nearby convenience store to buy some cigarettes. It was pouring with rain, and Mom became worried when he hadn't returned after several hours. She sent Garry and Jack out to look for him in case he'd maybe slipped and gotten hurt somehow, but there was no sign. Only later did we learn he had met a girlfriend outside the house who had driven over to pick him up and take him away. He and Mom divorced soon after.

None too soon, however. Billy left a shadow over our home long after he departed. While he was there, some kind of a cloud seemed to hang in the atmosphere. That's the only explanation I have for something I experienced multiple times when I was around three or four.

I'd wake in the night, fearful, and catch the flicker of the television out in the family room through my half-open bedroom doorway. Wanting to be comforted by my mom, I'd slip out of bed and head to the door to go and find her, only to be intercepted by some large presence.

It was a big, broad man, as far as I could tell in my half-asleep state, and though I couldn't detect his features, I wasn't scared. In fact, there was a calming, soothing aura about him. This figure would pick me up in his arms and say gently but firmly, "You can't go out there." Then he would put me back in bed, tuck me in, and stay close while I drifted off back to sleep. It all sounds quite fantastical, I realize, but this happened repeatedly enough over a period of time for me to be sure it really did take place and wasn't just a one-off fanciful dream. I never mentioned it to anyone.

Years later, I spoke about those experiences with Mom for the first time, and she nodded soberly. "There were some awful things going on in that house at that time," she told me. "Things that you did not need to see or know about."

While much of what was going on around me sexually as a young child thankfully went over my head, it somehow seemed to sensitize my heart. I developed an inner radar about people that offered a measure of protection. I had a gut sense of who not to be around alone—like the older male relative who came off all friendly and fun and offered me and the other kids candy. Only it was stashed in his front pant pockets, he said, and we would have to reach in there and get it for ourselves. Long before I understood about the birds and the bees, I knew to say no thanks.

Though a string of strange guys passed through our house, I only ever had one potential situation with any of them. I was asleep one night when I was awoken by an unknown man climbing into bed behind me. Startled, I asked him what he was doing, and he said sorry; he thought this was Mom's bed. That seemed a bit unlikely to me, given that we had only two bedrooms in the house, but who knows? Maybe he was still drunk. I told Mom about it the following day after the guy had left.

"Yeah," she said dismissively, "he told me he'd gotten into your bed by mistake."

Another occasion on which I dodged what could have been a more serious incident came about through Mom's next husband, Royce. We were over at his sister's house one time when we met his nephew. This guy was in his thirties, still living at home with his parents. He liked to go on different camping trips and would take underprivileged boys with him—something that these days would at least raise a few appropriately cautious eyebrows.

Not back then. Royce's nephew told me he was going to make a trip to a place in Arkansas where you could dig for diamonds, and would I like to go? It sure sounded like fun to me, never having even gone out of state, and no one questioned the idea, so off I went on a three-day trip with the guy, just twelve-year-old me and him.

I didn't think much about it when we ended up sleeping side by side in the back of his station wagon the first night; we were roughing it, after all. But as I lay there, he started to rub my back. Then, his hands began moving down my body. I bolted upright. "I've gotta go to the bathroom," I said without turning around. I climbed out of the vehicle, went to the bathroom, and then stretched out on the picnic table for the night. It was cool out there but safe.

The guy never mentioned anything the following morning, but I could tell he was irritated. He said I'd have to sleep in the station wagon with him that next night because it was going to be really cold. I told him I'd be okay, thanks. I also found some other teenagers at the campsite and hung out with them for most of the day. It was a long weekend, an awkward kind of standoff, but I got through it and got home without further incident.

I didn't escape all harm. As I've mentioned, violence was always in the air. I lived with an awareness that danger was only a wrong word away. That's why I was on constant alert at family gatherings: alcohol and anger were a highly combustible combination.

Mom may have been cold at times, but she wasn't cruel. I only ever recall her hitting me on a couple of occasions for some infraction. When she got mad, she'd typically throw a shoe at you, more as a signal to stop whatever we were doing than a serious attempt to actually strike us. I knew to be extra alert if she was wearing pumps when she got angry, though—those things could hurt if they landed.

> **VIOLENCE WAS ALWAYS IN THE AIR. I LIVED WITH AN AWARENESS THAT DANGER WAS ONLY A WRONG WORD AWAY.**

For the most part, the sense of danger was heightened by Mom's frequent absences more than her presence. Much as I loved Tracy, I knew I couldn't protect her if something terrible happened. Like the evening we were on our own when we heard some popping sounds from the house next door that sounded like gunshots.

We peered out the window as an ambulance and police cars raced up, their emergency lights illuminating the front yard. We couldn't make sense of all that was happening, but at one stage, I saw someone I recognized as the man who lived there being led out of the house in handcuffs and bundled into the back of one of the cop vehicles.

Other neighbors filled in the pieces of the puzzle the following day. The couple next door had separated; the guy was living in an apartment while the mom stayed at the house with their two daughters. When he discovered that his wife was having an affair, he went to the house and hid in a bedroom closet while she was out. When she came home with her boyfriend, the angry dad burst out on them and shot them both dead.

It was a little scary to think something so bad had happened just a few yards from us. When the two girls came back to the house with the police a couple of days later to collect their things, I remember seeing them through the window and thinking how sad it was that they now had neither a mom nor a dad.

That wasn't the only 911 drama that played out under our noses. When Cheryl was around sixteen, she became pregnant, but the relationship was rocky. She and the father had broken up, and she was staying at the house when he came over one night to try to patch things up. He was standing out in the backyard, waving a big knife and saying he would kill himself if Cheryl didn't take him back. There was some shouting back and forth, and then I watched through the window as the guy ran the blade down his stomach, blood going everywhere.

Someone called for an ambulance, and he was taken away and patched up. The whole thing shook me, but Mom wasn't impressed by the drama. "If the sorry son of a bitch had really wanted to kill himself, he'd have really stabbed himself deep rather than cut himself down from the belly button," she said dismissively. "Just being dramatic."

Growing up in an atmosphere of violence affected us all in different ways. Jack, especially, seemed to have an appetite for it. Cheryl learned to be tough in her own way. When I was around four or five, she got into a spat with another girl at school over a boy they were both sweet on. I don't recall who threw down the gauntlet, but the two of them met in a field after school to have it out. A bunch of kids showed up to watch, and the two girls went at each other, slapping and pulling each other's hair and rolling around on the ground. Cheryl came away as the winner, so she must have learned something from the family.

Being much younger than Garry and Jack, I didn't clash with them a great deal. But I knew to keep out of their way because they would get into it with each other occasionally. Jack was mean when he was drunk or high, and he was drunk or high often, so it was best not to cross him. Garry was typically more mellow. Except for one time.

By the time I was a high school senior, Garry's mental and emotional condition had deteriorated significantly. He'd had in-patient psychiatric care and was also tangled with the law. He would spend some time living on the streets or crashing on a friend's sofa for a few nights. Then, he would be back at our house from time to time.

Two days before my graduation, Garry was in the house when Mom told me she wanted the house cleaned and the laundry handled while she went out. I said okay, and when she left, I told Garry he needed to lend a hand. Somehow, that lit a fuse. Garry blew up in a way I had never seen before. He went crazy, launching himself at me and beating me with his fists. I tried to protect myself, but by the time he had finished, I was nursing a busted lip and two black eyes.

Mom and Royce, who had been out fishing, were horrified when they got back and saw the state I was in. When I told them what had happened, Royce began to go off on Garry. That only stirred him up again, and then Garry began beating on Royce. Mom called the cops, who arrived and took Garry away.

For my graduation, I made up a story about playing catch with my brothers and accidentally getting hit in the face by a baseball bat to explain away the cuts and bruises.

CHAPTER 8

The beloved children's television host Mr. Rogers once recalled how, when bad news made headlines when he was young, his mother said to him to "always look for the helpers." Because "if you look for the helpers, you will know there is hope," she told her son, to offer some comfort.[20]

Looking back with her words in mind, I see so many helpers on the fringes of my life, people who went out of their way to be kind to me when they didn't need to. But in doing so, they told me without saying directly that I mattered and was not entirely overlooked. They shined moments of light on some dark days.

I met several of these quiet encouragers at the Fireside Rec. I'd go there after school sometimes to hang out, but it became my home away from home during the summer. I'd be there six days a week from early morning until evening. I virtually lived there for several consecutive summers in my pre-teens.

There were several reasons for this. There were things to do there—a basketball court, a swimming pool, art classes. There were plenty of activities to pass the time, unlike back at the house where we had little to do and there might or might not be a TV set for some entertainment. On one occasion, the staff took a busload of us to see the Barnum & Bailey Circus. Going

---

[20] *Mister Rogers' Neighborhood*, Fred Rogers (February 19, 1968; Pittsburgh, PA: WQED Studios) Television.

on an outing was such a treat. I loved the whole event, from the animals to the clowns squeezed into their crazy little car. But maybe the best part of the entire trip was getting to eat cotton candy for the first time. Talk about a sugar rush.

Another big appeal of the Fireside Rec was its air conditioning—such a relief in the baking Texas summer months. We never had air conditioning at home: Mom said she didn't like how it made her feel dry-throated and sick. We made do with one box fan that we'd set in the window to draw in some slightly cooler outside air. Sometimes, it got so miserable at night that I'd strip down to my tighty-whities, spray myself all over with Off repellent, and take a blanket out and sleep outside on the porch in pursuit of some relief. The odd bug bite was better than the suffocating heat.

Even better than the Fireside Rec's AC was that there was food. Many of my friends were glad when school finished for the summer, but not me. I liked the lessons, but I liked the food we got there even more. When school was out, it could mean going hungry, so the snacks at the Fireside Rec were a big draw.

It must have been the summer of 1976 when I met Frank. That was the name tag in red stitching above the breast pocket on his gray janitor's overalls. Though he was probably in his sixties, a big burly guy with a bar-handle mustache and sizable gut, he was always approachable and friendly.

One day, I was in the activity room at lunchtime when I saw him through the hatchway, heating something in the microwave in the kitchen that was off-limits to us kids. It was a chicken pot pie, my absolute favorite meal, and a rare treat. When he had finished eating, I noticed the crust was left in the container he went to throw in the trash.

"Hey, Mister," I piped up, "are you gonna throw that away?"

"Yeah, why?"

"Coz that's the best part!"

He looked at me. "Do you want it?"

"Sure," I told him, gratefully receiving his leftovers. He watched as I scarfed it down.

"You know," he said, "I pretty much eat a pot pie every day, and I don't care a lot for the crust. So, any day you're here, you're welcome to it."

It became a standing appointment. I'd be sure to be in the activity room at his lunchtime; then, he'd eat his fill and pass the leftover crust to me. Most of the other kids were usually outside playing basketball, so it was our private transaction. We'd talk about this and that as I savored every mouthful of that wonderful, gravy-covered crust.

Did he really have a chicken pot pie every day for lunch as a matter of routine? Or did he decide he would after he saw how much I appreciated it? I don't know, but perhaps I will get to ask him one day. All I know for sure for now is that Frank's simple, caring gesture made a huge impact on me. And to this day, the crust of a chicken pot pie remains one of my favorite things to eat. Whenever Kim makes one for a family meal, my kids know to be sure to leave some of their crust and pass it over to me.

Then there was Fred, one of the activities staff. He was a muscular young guy who had played running back in college, tried to make it as a pro, and then turned to community service when that dream didn't work out. Fred made an impression on me not only because he was a rare Black face in our White community but also because he was easygoing and drove a Cutlass Supreme, a sweet car at the time.

Sometimes, if Frank wasn't around for any reason, Fred would ask me if I wanted to ride with him to go get lunch. Having grown up around some unsafe people, I had a pretty strong internal antenna when it came to people with ulterior motives, and there was none of that with Fred. He was just someone else going out of their way to be nice.

I don't know what protocols or policies we may have broken when we drove away from the center in his car, and I wonder what people thought at the local McDonald's and Jack-in-a-Box when we walked in together, this big Black guy and this skinny White kid—an unlikely pairing if ever there was one at that time—but I didn't care.

Bill was one of the older kids who often hung out at the Fireside Rec. He'd sit and eat his lunch out at one of the picnic benches facing the sports fields. He was in his mid-teens, like my older brothers, but unlike many of his peers who thought younger kids like me weren't cool to be around, he didn't seem to mind chatting with me when I would wander over to where he sat. Plus, he would nearly always have a bag of Doritos with him, and he'd let me have some.

Each of us with dark hair, brown eyes, and a dark complexion, Bill and I were not dissimilar. In fact, someone asked me if we were brothers one day, and in a burst of wishful thinking, I told them yes. Realizing this could get a little awkward, I told Bill jokingly what I had said. He laughed, said that was fine, and from then on always referred to me as his little brother. It made me feel good.

About eighteen months or so later, Bill stopped showing up. We'd never visited each other's homes; our friendship had been a purely Fireside Rec thing, so I asked my brothers if they knew what had happened to him because they were in the same year at school. Had he moved away or something?

Jack told me what had happened. Bill had been over at a friend's house, and they had been messing about with a pistol the other kid had. Bill thought all the bullets had been taken out, so, fooling around, he put the barrel to the side of his head, shouted, "Russian roulette!" and pulled the trigger. There was still a bullet in the chamber. The news of Bill's death left me feeling sick. The next time I was at the Fireside Rec, I wandered out to the bench where we had always met and sat down. I looked down at where he had etched "Bill was here" in the green-painted wood and cried, grateful for the mark he had also left in my life.

It wasn't only at the Fireside Rec that I encountered some little acts of kindness. I always knew I'd be treated well when I went to the nearby Fireside Grocery. My mouth would start to water as soon as I stepped inside and smelled the barbecued meats on offer in the popular local store and deli.

Once a month, when Mom got her food stamps, she'd give me one to treat myself, and I would head over to the Grocery. "So, it's that time of the month, is it?" Kenneth would say when he saw me coming in with my money. "Barbecue sandwich?" It always came with an extra serving of meat slapped on top, another private gesture I noticed from seeing how big other customers' orders were.

These sorts of splashes of goodness didn't just come from unexpected places; they also came from unlikely people. I'd grown accustomed to different men passing through the house. Though I didn't like it, I got used to tolerating them. Some I would see just once in the morning; they'd be sitting in the kitchen when I went to get my breakfast. On occasions, they would be there during the day on the weekends, and they would give Tracy and me each a quarter to go and buy some candy down at the store. This was big money for us, so we were excited. As an adult, I have to confess I suspect these episodes were more about getting us out of the house for a time rather than genuine interest in us.

> **THESE SORTS OF SPLASHES OF GOODNESS DIDN'T JUST COME FROM UNEXPECTED PLACES; THEY ALSO CAME FROM UNLIKELY PEOPLE.**

Buck was a guy who was around for a while. Because of him, we'd had a TV for one extended period—though when he and Mom broke up, he stopped making the rental payments, and we had to give it back.

I must have been around seven or so when I was telling Mom that I was having nightmares. Buck overheard our conversation and chipped in.

"You know what would keep you from having nightmares?" he asked. "Do you have a stuffed animal to sleep with?"

I told him no.

"Well, when I was a kid, I started having nightmares," he told me. "Then I started sleeping with a stuffed animal, and I didn't have those bad dreams no more. Why don't we go get you one?"

He loaded Mom, me, and Tracy into the car and drove us to the mall. When we walked into KB Toys, Buck told me, "Go find yourself a stuffed animal." I looked to him for some guidance.

"You'll know the right one," he said.

I settled on Honey Bunny, a giant stuffed rabbit with long, fluffy ears, his name emblazoned in red on a yellow jersey. Sure enough, Honey Bunny eased my nighttime fears, and he remained a comfort for more years than I care to admit, well into my teens. Years later, he would provide a sense of security for each of my five children when they were small.

Like with Frank, I don't know Buck's motives. Was he trying to impress my mom? Maybe. Or perhaps he saw something of himself in me, a small, fearful boy needing a token of reassurance that everything was going to be okay. We can't always be sure of people's motives; we just have to observe their actions. And in this small act of concern, Buck made a difference in my life.

If Fred, Frank, Bill, Kenneth, and others like them provided moments of warmth and light, the Stratton family was a long-term source of thoughtful sunshine through my teen years.

Scott and I met when I was riding past his house one day. It was one of the biggest and nicest in the neighborhood, and he was out in the front yard shooting hoops. I asked him if he wanted to take me on in a game, and he said sure, birthing probably the most enduring friendship of my life. Scott and I would navigate much of our crazy teenage years side by side.

Though we lived in different worlds financially, we were bonded by the absence of our fathers. Scott's dad, Chuck, was a lieutenant colonel in the US Air Force who went missing when his plane went down in a mission over Laos in 1971. We didn't spend a lot of time talking about our different losses—one a hero, one a hustler—but Scott did recall the last time he'd seen his dad. He had been returning to service after home leave when Scott had begged him not to go. I knew what it was like to have your father leave and never come back.

Scott never made an issue of our different circumstances, but we did all our hanging out together at his place. It had air conditioning, once again, and there was always a well-stocked fridge. They even had a microwave, which seemed really fancy to me. And I was amazed to discover they had Ovaltine in the cupboard like it was no big deal. I loved it, but Mom would never buy it for us because it was too expensive. I always had a glass when I was over at Scott's, sipping and savoring it like fine wine.

Stocky and more athletic than me—he trounced me in that first game of basketball—Scott was also a good baseball player who participated in summer leagues. I'd always tag along to watch him play, with the bonus of knowing that his mom might take us out for dinner or ice cream afterward.

A WHOLE LIFE

All the young guys in the community agreed Sallie Stratton was the hot mom, but I also knew her as the tenderhearted mom. Many years later, I would learn that whenever she, Scott, and his two brothers were doing something, she would always suggest he invite me along, too. I still remember going to the movies with them to see *Jaws*,[21] *Close Encounters of the Third Kind*,[22] and *Alien*.[23] It was quite a novel experience to actually get a ticket! Mrs. Stratton always paid for everything without making me feel awkward about it.

I had my first Arby's with the Strattons. When Scott told me we were going out to get a roast beef sandwich, I wasn't too keen because all I knew was the cheap, gristly cuts Mom sometimes served up at home. I was blown away by my experience, adding Arby's to chicken pot pie, and later Whataburger, as my favorite eats.

The Strattons even took me on my first-ever vacation. They often went on big trips as a family—Hawaii, Mexico—and one summer, they invited me to go to Padre Island. I was beyond excited: I'd only ever been out of state once with my stepfather's relative, and that had not been a good experience. The idea of traveling four hundred miles away to spend two weeks at the beach seemed amazing.

There was one snag. I was worried about not having enough changes of clothes. Thankfully, Mom found a little extra money from somewhere, and I was able to buy my first-ever pair of

---

21 Steven Spielberg, *Jaws* (June 20, 1975; Hollywood, CA: Universal Pictures).
22 Steven Spielberg, *Close Encounters of the Third Kind* (November 16, 1977; Culver City, CA: Columbia Pictures).
23 Ridley Scott, *Alien* (May 25, 1979; Los Angeles, CA: 21st Century Fox).

swimming trunks—I usually just wore cut-off jeans—plus a couple of tee-shirts and a pair of flip-flops. I was stoked.

Actually, there was a second problem. I knew we would spend our time hanging out at the pool and the beach, so on the drive out, I had to confess to Scott that I didn't know how to swim. Mom had always been terrified of the water, and as she had never encouraged me to learn, I had inherited some of her nervousness. But I knew I had to get over it. We broke the drive to Padre Island at a mom-and-pop hotel in La Grange. It had a small swimming pool, where Scott and his younger brother, Steven, gave me some rudimentary lessons, enough that I could float and keep my head above water.

It was an incredible couple of weeks. We stayed in a condo right on the ocean. Scott, his brothers, and I hung out with all the other teenagers during the day, and in the evening, his mom would take us out to eat. I still remember the fresh-caught shrimp bowls. After two glorious, tanned, and well-fed weeks, it was back to basics in Pleasant Grove. But I carried the memory of living what to me seemed to be the rich life, another thread in my tapestry of hope.

CHAPTER 9

When they hear my story and I tell people I've never had therapy nor taken any prescription medications, some people are amazed. How could I have experienced all I did and not been deeply affected by it in some way? I put it down to several things—God's love and care, the support of others, my personality, and some of the good things I inherited from both my parents.

Yes, they fell short in many ways, but they also passed on some things that I have been able to use for good—an outgoing nature, resilience, and an entrepreneurial spirit. They may have employed these in less than positive ways, but those qualities in and of themselves are full of potential and possibility. It's all about in what direction you choose to channel them.

Even given all that I went through, I wouldn't change the past in any way. That might seem hard to believe, but I look at it this way: all those situations and circumstances were part of the journey that brought me to where I am today. Without them, I would not have an amazing wife, a wonderful family, and a rewarding career. In light of that, those past difficulties and problems are a price worth paying.

One lesson I learned both from watching the way Mom lived and from my own experiences was not to try to hold on to things too tightly. Instead, enjoy them while you have the opportunity because you never know what tomorrow will bring. It's important to live in the moment and understand that neither good nor bad times last forever. As someone once said, life happens! It's up to us how we will respond to the blessings and the burdens.

Two particular examples of learning to hold things lightly come to mind. The first was not long after I'd spent the weekend with Dad, and I was still surfing on the high of that special time before the letdown came. Life seemed pretty good, except for one thing. The new school year was due to start soon, and I was getting to the age when I was more aware of how important it was to fit in—which wasn't easy when you didn't have as much money as other people.

Now, we may have been dirt poor, but we were never dirty. People might have been able to tell we had no money, but they couldn't smell we had no money. Mom made sure of that. Our old clothes were always clean, not like some kids at school who had that funky, sour odor about them because they repeatedly wore the same old, unwashed things.

> **PEOPLE MIGHT HAVE BEEN ABLE TO TELL WE HAD NO MONEY, BUT THEY COULDN'T SMELL WE HAD NO MONEY.**

Still, I was starting to realize that wearing the same old few sets of clothes made me stand out at school, not in a good way. With my hormones rising, I was beginning to notice girls and recognize how you dressed made an impression, for good or bad. I had jeans with holes in them before they were fashionable. I didn't so much mind that what I wore was old, but when I outgrew what we had, it was apparent we were poor because my pants were too short. I so badly wanted some new clothes for school, not the best pickings we could find at Goodwill or The Salvation Army, as usual.

It seemed like Christmas and birthday all rolled into one, then, when a few days before fourth grade started, Mom told me someone was coming to the house to take me shopping for some new school clothes. Say what! I don't know whether Mom had applied for some assistance, or our names had come up through school circles, or something like that, but a nice lady came around the Friday before the new school year and took me to Riley Ready to Wear, a clothing store in the area.

I'd been there a couple of times, but only to look. It wasn't a high-end fashion kind of place, but everything was new. I would marvel that people got to buy that kind of stuff without even thinking about it. It was hard to believe I was there now to do just that. I came out with two pairs of Levis, two shirts, a pair of shoes, and, most thrillingly of all, a Levi jean jacket. All brand new. I'd never experienced anything like it. I couldn't wait to try my new things on, but Mom insisted I wait until the first day of school. I was counting the hours.

Saturday night was quite special because, for some reason, Mom decided to have a rare evening at home with us. We were sitting there watching television when Mom detected the smell of smoke. She went into my and Tracy's bedroom and came running back into the living room. "Come on, we've got to get out of here. There's a fire in the closet!"

Oh no: that was where all my new clothes were hanging and stored. Garry and Jack started trying to get water from the sink to put out the flames while I headed to the bedroom to rescue my prized new things, but Mom pulled us all away and out of the house. We stood in the driveway waiting for the fire department to arrive, swirling flames and smoke visible through the windows.

The fire wasn't bad enough to damage the interior too severely, but the flames were hot enough, and the smoke was thick enough to ruin everything in the cupboard. All my new clothes were gone, and never even worn outside the store's dressing room. I was heartbroken.

I spent a sleepless couple of nights on a neighbor's couch while Tracy was taken in by another family up the street, and Jack and Garry, who had been home at the time, found a place to crash at friends' homes. Then Mom found another house to rent a couple of streets away, and we salvaged what was left of our things and moved over. When I made it to school for the new year, it was once again in the best secondhand finds we had been able to make.

Years later, Mom told me she discovered soon after the fire that Tracy had started it accidentally. She'd been playing with a box of matches in our bedroom when she struck one, and it burned her finger. Startled, she'd thrown it away from her into the cupboard, where it had set fire to something. Mom kept those details from me because she didn't want me to be mad at my sister.

In some ways, that crushing experience prepared me for what came soon after, on my eleventh birthday. I desperately wanted a bicycle: All my friends had one, and I envied the independence and freedom that came with those two wheels. I told Mom that's what I wanted more than anything for my birthday, but I didn't hold out too much hope because she was single-momming life at that time, and money was tighter than usual. It wouldn't be the first time a birthday came and went without a gift—though she did usually make me a German chocolate cake, my favorite.

So, I was as excited as I had just about ever been when I woke up to find a green-and-yellow bicycle sitting in the living room for me. It was used, but I didn't care. It was a bicycle and a ten-speeder, just like I had wanted. My birthday fell on the weekend, so with no school, I spent all day out, cycling around.

I was so excited I didn't want to waste any time, so I came home briefly at lunchtime and ate a self-made sandwich real fast—Mom was out somewhere with Evelyn—then hopped back on my bike. Wolfing the food down like that and then rushing out again didn't sit too well with me: somewhere down the street, I passed out. I came to laying on the ground next to my bike, knees and elbows scraped. A quick trip back home to put some Band-Aids on, and I was back out pedaling again. I finally came home when it was dark, a bit bruised and tired, but happy.

With Mom out for the evening with Evelyn, as usual, that left me and Tracy at home with Jack and Garry, who were both living with us then. I was hanging out with them in the family room when one of their friends dropped by to tell them a wild story.

"You're not going to believe what happened to me yesterday!" he said. "I'm out on my bike last night when I stop by some woods to go take a leak. As I'm standing there by a tree, I look back and see two women pull up by my bike in a car. They get out, throw my bike into the trunk, and drive off with it before I can zip my pants up and run out to stop them."

"That's crazy," Jack said. "Where did this happen?"

"Just up the street from here."

"What color is your bike?"

"Yellow and green. Why?"

There was an awkward silence. Then Jack turned to me. "Hey, Jackie Wayne, go get your bicycle and bring it out here."

With a sinking feeling, I went out to the rear porch where I'd leaned my new pride and joy against the wall and wheeled it into the room.

"What the . . .," exclaimed my brother's friend. "That's my bike! What are you doing with it?"

"Hey, you've got to give it back," said Jack.

"No!" I wailed. "It's mine!"

"No, it's not, Jackie Wayne," Jack insisted. "It's his. You've got to give it back."

I knew he was right, but it broke my heart. I shed some big tears after Jack's friend left with my—his—bike. When Mom came home, I told her what had happened. "Mom!" I sobbed. "You stole that bike. . . ."

She was unrepentant and seemingly unmoved by my loss: "Look at it this way: at least you had it for a day, right?"

Growing up without money, you become very aware of how powerless you are when you don't have any. Though Mom would give us a little cash now and then as a special treat, we never got a regular allowance. When I learned that my friend Scott was given money every week for keeping his room clean and doing a few chores, I asked Mom whether I could have an allowance, too.

"Yeah," she said. "I'll allow you to live at home." And that was the end of that.

Early on, I decided that I didn't want to be dependent on other people's charity or generosity; I wanted to be able to provide for myself. I started mowing lawns when I was in sixth grade. It wasn't exactly a sophisticated operation; we didn't have a lawn mower of our own, so anyone who agreed to let me cut their grass for a buck also had to let me use their equipment. I wonder how many of those who took me on when I knocked on their door, looking poor and hopeful, were doing me more of a service than I was providing for them.

> **EARLY ON, I DECIDED THAT I DIDN'T WANT TO BE DEPENDENT ON OTHER PEOPLE'S CHARITY OR GENEROSITY; I WANTED TO BE ABLE TO PROVIDE FOR MYSELF.**

Mowing lawns in the Dallas summer heat wasn't the sweetest gig, so I was pleased when I got a job busing tables at the Canton Diner. The owners of the little mom-and-pop eatery paid me

$1.50 an hour, and I also got to eat some of the leftover food that would have otherwise just been thrown out, so that felt like a really sweet deal. From there, I progressed to Pantry Pride, a convenience store where I helped stock the shelves. Then it was back to the kitchen, this time as a dishwasher at the Catfish Inn.

Though things were tight at home, Mom never required me to give her any of my earnings. It did feel good to be able to do something for her occasionally, however. Some evenings, I'd tell her I would provide dinner and bring home a bucket of chicken or something like that. My time at the Catfish Inn turned out to be rewarding: every Thursday night, they offered an all-you-can-eat catfish and frog legs buffet, and I got to take home some of what was surplus at the end of the night.

I'd use some of the money I made to buy Tracy little things she wanted but Mom couldn't afford; Tracy was too young to be working and I enjoyed being able to provide for her. The rest of my earnings went to buying some nicer clothes for myself and then to what was a growing source of escape for me: music.

Having older siblings, I'd been introduced to music at an early age. Garry and Jack were hard rock fans, and at one stage, we all shared a room where I was introduced to Led Zeppelin and Pink Floyd. But that wasn't all I heard. I was about five when Cheryl came home one day with a 45 she was really excited about. "You've got to listen to this song," she told us all. I didn't understand a word of what Don McLean was singing about in "American Pie,"[24] but something about that song captivated me.

---

[24] Don McLean, vocalist, "American Pie," by Don McLean, released October, 1971, track 1 on *American Pie*, United Artists.

A WHOLE LIFE

Music also became a big part of my relationship with Scott. It gave us a common language and put words and melodies to emotions we didn't always understand as teenage boys growing into our bodies and personalities. We'd hang out in his room, where he had his own record player, a classy Emerson, with the volume cranked up. Scott would use part of his weekly allowance to buy new albums. We'd walk down to the local Eckerd's, a few blocks from his house, to choose one of the latest releases available in the music section at the back of the store.

I still remember the first LP I ever bought with my own money. Cheryl had moved out and was living independently, and she gave me five bucks to go over and mow her grass. I used my payment to get a copy of Fleetwood Mac's *Rumors*,[25] still one of my all-time favorite albums.

If listening to music was a revelation, hearing it played live was like a revolution. The first concert Scott and I went to was at the Tarrant County Convention Center in Dallas-Fort Worth in 1977. When he asked if I wanted to go, I demurred because I didn't have enough money for a ticket, but true to form, he said he would pay because he didn't want to go alone. His mom dropped us off there, and Blue Oyster Cult, Head East, and The Johnny Van Zandt Band made our ears ring and our pulses pound.

From then on, we attended all the shows we could. Among them, the following year, was the first-ever Texas Jam at the Cotton Bowl. The lineup for the all-day outdoor event was a rock fan's dream list: Van Halen, Eddie Money, Journey, Heart, Ted Nugent, Aerosmith, and more. Alcohol flowed, and the air

---

25 Fleetwood Mac, *Rumors*, Warner Bros., 1977, https://en.wikipedia.org/wiki/Rumours_(album), Jan. 9, 2024.

was thick with the smell of weed. Scott and I didn't drink or smoke anything—that would come later—but we took in the whole hard-partying vibe. With something like eighty thousand people crammed into the stadium in temperatures well over one hundred degrees, it was a sweat-bath of a day, kids passing out left and right from heatstroke.

IF LISTENING TO MUSIC WAS A REVELATION, HEARING IT PLAYED LIVE WAS LIKE A REVOLUTION.

For a few hours, concerts meant I could get lost in the shared sounds and senses, forgetting the chaos and disorder that awaited me at home.

CHAPTER 10

I smoked weed for the first time when I was ten. With Mom. I'd seen her with the occasional joint before, though she didn't do drugs much. They were a part of the mix in our family gatherings, along with alcohol, but she didn't want to get caught up in the hard drugs world, and neither did she want to have to pay for them when she got her drinks bought for her. A striking woman with more than a passing resemblance to Loretta Lynn, she was never short of a guy or two willing to pay the bar tab.

Evelyn was over one evening before they headed out to the bar, and the two of them were sitting in the kitchen when she pulled a joint out of her purse and lit up. They passed it between themselves as I watched.

"You wanna try it?" Evelyn asked me.

I looked over at Mom, expecting her to chew her friend out for the suggestion. Instead, she just shrugged.

"Go for it, if you want," she told me. "Might as well try it here. You're going to try it at some point anyway."

I'd sipped different relatives' drinks at parties before, but I'd never smoked anything, so I didn't really know what to do. I made a real mess of the joint as I tried to purse my lips around it and inhale.

A WHOLE LIFE

"No, no, no," Evelyn said. "Here, let me show you something fun." Then she took a big hit, held it long, and whispered, "Come here" out of the corner of her mouth.

I went over to her, and she took my face in her hands. Then she put her mouth against mine, parted my lips with her fingers, and exhaled into my mouth. It felt weird and wonderful all at the same time. My head seemed to float, and my body sagged.

"Well," Mom said, "how do you feel?"

"Kinda funny."

"Yeah, that's the way it's supposed to be. It makes you feel better about things."

Not long after that, I became a semi-regular user, usually smoking with my brothers and later my friends—and on a couple more occasions with Mom. Something in me knew to draw the line at hard drugs, though—I turned down offers from Jack and Garry to try LSD, coke, and heroin.

I discovered that marijuana took the edge off some of the sharp corners of my life. When I was a little stoned, I didn't care so much that we were poor. I didn't mind wearing old clothes. And while some people experience "the munchies" when they use pot, a heightened appetite, I found that it somehow soothed my hunger pangs. Going to bed with an empty stomach when you were pretty mellow didn't seem quite so bad. And listening to my brothers' music, like Pink Floyd's *Dark Side of the Moon*,[26] was much more interesting when you were high.

Despite all the pluses, I drew a hard line for myself about using pot. I swore to myself that I would never go to school high.

---

[26] Pink Floyd, *Dark Side of the Moon*, Harvest, Capitol, March 1, 1973, https://en.wikipedia.org/wiki/The_Dark_Side_of_the_Moon, Jan. 9, 2024.

From junior high on, there was always a group of stoners out on the school grounds, smoking weed during recess, but I would never join them. It just seemed too disrespectful to the staff to show up to class wasted.

Having started smoking dope pretty young, I was almost a latecomer to alcohol. Like I said, I'd tasted beer, vodka, and whiskey here and there but never enjoyed it. Then, when Scott and I were twelve, we decided it was time to find out what getting drunk felt like so we could compare it to being high.

His mom and grandmother had a well-stocked drinks cabinet in the dining room, so he snuck down there and plucked a bottle of whiskey from the collection. Hiding it under his clothes, he slipped out of the house, where I met him on the sidewalk. As we walked away to find somewhere to start drinking, the bottle fell from his grasp, shattering on the concrete.

Scott went back to liberate some more liquor. I don't remember what kind of bottle he came back with, but we walked around swigging the contents. We started to swagger, then we began to laugh and giggle, and we finished by throwing up all over the sidewalk. Somehow, I managed to weave my way home, get to my room without anyone noticing me, and pass out on the bed.

The next day, I was back over at Scott's house, both of us nursing sick stomachs and thick heads. Joining his mom and grandma for dinner, we tried not to give away the fact that we were both feeling pretty sick. Then his grandma said to his mom there seemed to be a couple of bottles missing from the drinks cabinet, and did she know anything about that? They almost fell out about it while Scott and I sat there trying to look innocent.

That first serious drinking session wasn't bad enough to put me off completely. Some months later, Scott and I were invited to a party where his older brother, Charles, was playing with his band. We were younger than everyone else there, but they didn't give us a hard time about that. This time, I tried beer and discovered a buzz I liked. Whereas marijuana mellowed me out, beer made me feel more outgoing, more up. I liked it. Over time, I'd learn how to balance the two for just the right kind of mood, not too laid back but not too crazy either.

Both of us having older siblings made it easier for Scott and me to get hold of weed and booze. By the time I was fifteen, I was buying alcohol myself from the liquor store with some of my wages; having grown a full mustache helped. One night, I was driving Scott and myself back to his place in his mom's car after some serious drinking when we got pulled over by the police. There was no way I was going to pass a sobriety test. This was a serious situation.

"You boys been drinking?" the cop asked as he lowered his head by my driver's window.

I started to say no when he cut me off. "Come on, fellas," he said. "I can smell it on you. Been drinking?"

"Yes, sir."

"Where are you headed?"

"To his house," I said, pointing to Scott in the passenger seat.

"How far is that?"

"Five or six miles from here?"

"I tell you what," the police officer said. "If you promise me you're going to go straight home, I'll let you go, okay?"

Vowing to do just that, Scott and I both breathed a huge sigh of relief, and I very cautiously drove us back to Scott's house.

This wasn't the only pass we got on a run-in with the law. When Scott bought a copy of AC/DC's new *Back in Black*, we picked up a six-pack, put the cassette in the car stereo, and cranked up the volume.

We'd pulled over behind a warehouse to take a leak when a police car drove up alongside us and parked. The two officers were young guys, and we apologized for peeing out in public, hoping we could wriggle out of the situation.

"Hey, is that the new AC/DC album?" one asked.

"Yeah."

"Well, I've only heard a song or two on the radio. Turn it up."

We did, and then the other cop asked what we were drinking. He didn't believe me when I said nothing.

"Michelob," I admitted.

"Well, get us one!" he said.

Equal parts surprised and relieved, I dug out a can for each of them, and the four of us sat on the hood of the car for an hour or more, sipping beer and listening to AC/DC. Then, there was a call on their radio, and one of them said they had to respond.

"Be safe now," he cautioned. "Thanks for letting us listen. And thanks for the beer."

Drink, drugs, and rock-n-roll may have been able to distract me for a moment, an evening, but they didn't fill the hole I sensed getting wider deep inside me, the feeling of something missing. I hoped that maybe sex could do that.

Having shared many teenage firsts with Scott, it seemed appropriate that we each had our earliest sexual encounters at the same time. In due time, my first full sexual experience was a bit like my first serious encounters with drink and drugs: *Huh, is this what all the fuss is about? Doesn't seem as great as it's been cracked up to be.* But just like with alcohol and weed, there was enough promise, enough pull, for me to want to keep experimenting. And, sure enough, as I kept exploring, I discovered something that made me feel really alive—at least fleetingly.

> **DRINK, DRUGS, AND ROCK-N-ROLL MAY HAVE BEEN ABLE TO DISTRACT ME FOR A MOMENT, AN EVENING, BUT THEY DIDN'T FILL THE HOLE I SENSED GETTING WIDER DEEP INSIDE ME, THE FEELING OF SOMETHING MISSING.**

I also found that I had a gift for sweet-talking girls into giving me what I wanted, which I shamelessly exploited. Having grown up in an environment that had me on high alert, always attuned to people around me, I could read a room pretty well. I could identify those girls who might be susceptible to some smooth words. I never dreamt of mistreating a girl physically, but I didn't realize how I was using them emotionally. I set the rules for the relationship: they dated just me, but I could date whoever I wanted. And I embraced Uncle Sonny's philosophy: if I wanted their opinion, I gave it to them.

My attitude and actions didn't seem wrong to me at the time. As far as I knew from the way the people around me had always acted, sex was just a casual thing, almost inconsequential—no big deal. So, I never dated anyone for too long, always looking for a new challenge, a new conquest. At least, that's what I thought I was pursuing: now I realize I was actually chasing something deeper, seeking some kind of connection that the mere physical act could never deliver. After the pleasure, I'd feel empty rather than satisfied. I realized I didn't really love these girls, whatever I may have told them. A small voice inside said, *You shouldn't be doing this, Jack.*

CHAPTER 11

When Mom married Royce Jameson, some years after her divorce from Billy, it was a mixed blessing. It meant she wasn't out at a bar until two or three o'clock in the morning, leaving me and Tracy to fend for ourselves, so that was good. But the trade-off was the effect of their volatile relationship.

Things were pretty nice to begin with. They met in a bar, unsurprisingly, and Royce wanted to make a good impression on Tracy and me. When he came round to take Mom out to a movie, he asked if we wanted to go along too, which we thought was just the greatest. With a good job as a manager of a supplies warehouse, Royce dressed well and drove a decent car, no clunker. He also lived in a house of his own that was way smarter than ours, across town in a better neighborhood.

Moving there when he and Mom married took me away from some of my old haunts, but it introduced me to a new delight: Whataburger. Whenever Mom gave me a little money for a treat, I would take myself off there for a burger, fries, and soda. I'd linger over my meal, watching the families eating happily together and wishing my life could be like that.

A year or so after he and Mom married, Royce had asked if he could legally adopt Tracy and me. We were so excited: it felt like we finally had a real father. We had to go down to the courthouse in downtown Dallas to make it official, and they took us out for lunch to celebrate after. I remember thinking how good it felt to have an actual dad and a legal last name of my own.

Being with Royce also meant a little more money to spare, and for my thirteenth birthday, I finally got my own bike. I desperately wanted a red Huffy like all the cool kids rode, but that was too much of a stretch. But I got a red knockoff version from Sears, and it was new, and it was all mine. That was too much to be happy about to feel bad. I rode that thing hard for the next year. Then, one morning, it was missing from where I used to wedge it between the fence and the side of our shed. I shrugged the loss off, grateful for having had my bike for as long as I did.

I don't pretend to know all Royce's motives for adopting us, but later, I'd wonder whether part of the reason was because he and Mom thought it might help reduce the support he had to pay for two kids from his previous marriage. When he and Mom eventually divorced, I heard no more from or about Royce for a long time. Then, a few years ago, I got a letter out of the blue from an attorney. It informed me that Royce had died, and Tracy and I had been included in his will: we each received a $10 money order.

I didn't know whether to feel touched or ticked by the gesture until an attorney I knew speculated that Royce had left us that token amount to fulfill an obligation and prevent us from contesting the inheritance. Speculating wasn't going to help me. Deciding to let go of any resentment, I used the money to buy two lottery tickets, thinking it would be fun if Royce became the one who made me a millionaire.

That daydream failed to materialize—just as had the prospect of a happy new home when Mom and Royce first got together. To begin with, he was easygoing. He enjoyed camping and fishing, so in the early days, we'd all go on fun weekend trips. But I began to realize that he had a Jekyll and Hyde kind of personality; you just had to know which one you were dealing with.

> **DECIDING TO LET GO OF ANY RESENTMENT, I USED THE MONEY TO BUY TWO LOTTERY TICKETS, THINKING IT WOULD BE FUN IF ROYCE BECAME THE ONE WHO MADE ME A MILLIONAIRE.**

He wasn't physically abusive, just mentally. He seemed to like controlling us. When he got home from work, he'd spend the evening in front of the television, chain-smoking. He would take the TV guide we got and circle all the shows he wanted to see—which just happened to be at the same time as my favorites. He'd even watch the same shows over and over again, seemingly just for the sake of it. There were weeks when he wouldn't even speak to us, hardly acknowledging our existence.

The meanest thing he did was with his snacks. At the store, he would buy things we were not allowed to eat. He'd write his name on packets of chips and warn us not to touch them. He especially loved Babe Ruth bars, and Tracy and I would badger him to let us have a bite. He hated sharing, so when he got a bar out from wherever he secretly kept them, he'd open it in front of us and then lick the length of it before wrapping it up again. That sure put us off ever trying to sneak a mouthful when he wasn't looking.

Meanwhile, he and Mom would fight like cat and dog. They'd go into their bedroom, and we would hear shouting and the sounds of things being thrown. Tracy and I would turn up the volume on the television to drown out the fighting. When they emerged, Mom might have a red mark on her face, and Royce would have scratches on his. As time went on, he'd disappear for a few days to a hotel and then come back when things had cooled down. Soon enough, it would all start over again.

One saving grace was that, as I was getting older, I could spend more time away from home. But any sense of equilibrium I had was upended when I was a sophomore, and Mom announced that we were moving to Louisiana.

I'd heard her and Royce talking about it as a way of getting out of the child support he was having to pay to his previous wife, which was reducing what he was bringing home, but I'd not thought it was a serious plan. Another draw for Mom was that it would take her back to the state of her childhood and close to where a cousin lived.

When I found out they were serious, I was alarmed. Sure, we'd moved around and lived in a string of different houses while I was growing up, but they had always been within the same area. We'd known the same people and frequented the same stores, and I had attended the same schools with all my friends. The worst part was the thought of being separated from my best friend, Scott. Mom tried to sweeten the prospect by explaining how much better off we'd be there and how we'd live in a really nice house. Like so many other promises, this turned out to be untrue.

Despite my reluctance, I actually found myself enjoying some aspects of our new situation. The house they were going to buy in Ruston fell through, so we ended up in a rental in Jonesboro, where I attended the large high school. But after a couple of months, Mom and Royce found a new place to buy in Quitman, about a half hour away.

This turned out to be a good thing for me. With less than a thousand residents, Quitman didn't have a high school of its own; students K through 12 all shared the same campus. With only thirty or so students in my class and arriving midway through the school year, I stood out a bit from the first day. And when the other kids learned I'd come from big-city Dallas to their small town—one stop light and one convenience store—they thought I was pretty cool. Well, the girls did, at least, because they associated it with *Dallas*,[27] the hit TV series of the time. "Do you know JR?" they'd ask teasingly.

Some of the guys weren't so welcoming to the new boy who was turning some heads. One came up to me and said, "There's only two things that come out of Texas. That's steers and queers: and I don't see any horns on you...." I laughed him off, trying to avoid a confrontation. I'd seen how most of the guys arrived at school in trucks with their hunting rifles slung casually in

---

27 *Dallas*, Leonard Katzman, et. al. (April 2, 1978; Los Angeles, CA: CBS), Television.

A WHOLE LIFE

the back—I felt like I'd landed in an episode of *The Dukes of Hazzard*.[28] I figured it was best to try to keep my head down.

That approach worked, and in due course, I was an accepted part of the scene. I got invited to all the parties, and I worked my way through a good number of the freshman and second-year high school girls.

Life at home didn't get any better, however. In fact, it got worse when it became clear that this "new life" wasn't going to be so great. That had been evident even within a few days of arriving: the police showed up at the door and took Royce away for failure to pay child support. So much for wriggling out of that responsibility. When he came back, it was with an agreement that his wages would be garnished.

To make matters worse, he had not been able to find a job with income equal to what he was earning back in Dallas. He ended up with an entry-level gig at the local paper mill, from which a mildewy smell emanated and hung over the whole town. It was the community's main employer; families had worked there for generations. As a newcomer, Royce worked swing shifts: one week from midnight to 8:00 a.m., the next from 7:00 a.m. to 3:00 p.m. That threw his sleep pattern off, which only made him grumpier.

Reduced income meant a lot of beans and cornbread again. We couldn't afford a great place to live: the house had a dull Army green exterior and no central air, so we sweated through the summers. In the winter, it got really cold because you could see outside through gaps in the wall slats. We had one propane heater to try to warm the whole place. It was so shabby that I

---

28 *Dukes of Hazzard*, Paul Baxlet, et. al. (January 26, 1979; Los Angeles, CA: CBS), Television.

never invited friends over; I always went to their place. And if anyone ever gave me a ride home, I always had them drop me at the top of the street so they didn't get to see where I actually lived.

Like in Dallas, I had some kind families take me under their wing. One of the good friends I made was David Schmidt, whose mom was a great cook and very friendly. I'd go over there sometimes even if I knew David wasn't around, just to be able to spend some time with his mom. One of her specialties was deer meat chili. She would call me to say she had a pot readying on the stove, and I would go over to eat some and chat with her.

I started out as a fairly diligent student but had let school take a back seat to girls and partying by the time I was a junior. If beer made me feel like Superman, Bacardi 151 was my Kryptonite. One time, I woke up after too much of that high-proof rum with a girl's class ring wedged onto my finger, cigarette burns all over my hand, and no idea where either had come from. On another occasion, I ended up standing on a table and vowing to fight all-comers. This from a scrawny kid who had only ever been in two fights (one with Darla, the fourth-grade girl bully, who had knocked the stuffing out of me).

I kept my pledge of not going to school drunk or high, but there were a few days when I turned up a little hungover or headachy. If I stood out to the teachers at all, it was probably because I was a bit of a jokester, always looking to make people laugh. I was more disruptive than diligent. Which is why I was so surprised when Miss McCarthy, the English teacher, came up to me at the end of class one day in my senior year and told me she wanted me to take the lead in the annual school play. This was a pretty big tradition in a small school, and I'd never done any kind of drama before, nor really shown much aptitude in class. I was also intimidated by the idea of actually having to do some work and memorize all those lines. I told her no thanks; it wasn't for me.

> **IF I STOOD OUT TO THE TEACHERS AT ALL, IT WAS PROBABLY BECAUSE I WAS A BIT OF A JOKESTER, ALWAYS LOOKING TO MAKE PEOPLE LAUGH. I WAS MORE DISRUPTIVE THAN DILIGENT.**

"Look, Jack, just think about it overnight," she said. "I can't make you do it, of course, but I think you can do this. Let me know tomorrow: if you still don't want to, I'll pick someone else."

Something about the fact that she believed in me, that she had seen something, stuck with me. I went home and told Mom what Miss McCarthy wanted me to do and how I wasn't sure.

"Well, she wouldn't have picked you if she didn't think you could do it," she said, unexpectedly encouraging.

The next day, I went and told Miss McCarthy that I was in. Once I had committed myself, I was rather daunted when I got a copy of the script, a comedy, and discovered just how many lines I had to learn. But there was an incentive. I learned that the female character would be played by one of the best-looking senior girls in the school. She was way out of my league, only dating college kids because she thought high schoolers were beneath her. However, the two main characters we played got to share a kiss, so we had to do some rehearsing!

For the first time in as long as I could remember, I applied myself to studying. I discovered that I enjoyed the process of preparation and learning about how to move on stage to make an impact. Still, I was very nervous on opening night, especially when I looked out and saw Mom and Tracy in the second row, sitting there looking proud.

When I made my entrance, and my first line drew a chorus of laughter, I had a rush unlike anything I had experienced. I sailed through the rest of the night, loving how it felt to hold people's attention and channel their mood. To put a bow on things, afterward, Mom came up and told me that I had done a great job—a rare and meaningful compliment.

We got to perform the play again for the younger students in the school the next day. Buzzed by the way things had gone the night before, we cut loose a little and had fun making the kids laugh, improvising a fair amount. Again, I made a note of how it felt to touch people's emotions through sharing a story. I didn't see drama in my future in any way, but I tucked away the affirmation of being noticed and appreciated and the satisfaction of enriching people's lives.

CHAPTER 12

We weren't a religious family by any means. Mom believed in God in a vague kind of way, that there must be a big Someone or Something behind everything in this world, but she didn't have much time for religious people. Occasionally, we'd have folks knock at the door and invite us to their local church, and she would always get rid of them as quickly as she could. Judgmental do-gooders, she would tell us. Looking down on poor people like us.

We never went to church as a family, but I attended some of the summer Bible camps for kids that were hosted in the area. Despite her negative feelings, Mom never stopped me from going—apart from anything else, it gave me something to do during the school vacation, and we also got to enjoy the free snacks. To be honest, the goodies were one of the main attractions for me.

I liked some of the stories we were told, though, especially the one about Daniel being thrown into the lions' den and coming out without a scratch the following day because God had protected him. I also enjoyed the one about his three friends who were tied up and tossed into a blazing furnace but emerged without even singed clothing. At the time, these were just exciting stories, but in hindsight, I wonder if they spoke to me on a deeper level: like Daniel and his friends, I'd been exposed to great danger but somehow came through unscathed. Someone was looking out for me, like those nights when I had been gently prevented from wandering out of my bedroom.

Certainly, I associated church with a special kind of peace. There was a Baptist church not far from where we lived in Dallas that, like some other churches back then, never locked its doors. When I was out of the house during the day, just kicking around with nothing to do, I'd often slip inside and sit in one of the pews. Alone in the sanctuary, I'd look at the cross on the wall and enjoy the stillness. My visits came to an end one day when the church burned down: Jack would later boast of having started the fire with some of his friends.

Though I wouldn't have considered myself religious in any way, I had some experiences that I knew were otherworldly in addition to those encounters with that large figure in my bedroom. I began to have dreams that I knew were of a spiritual nature, though I couldn't really make any sense of them. They were powerful enough, though, for me to be moved to write them down when I woke up so I wouldn't forget them.

The first was when I was in sixth grade and featured Babe, my favorite of all the raggedy dogs we had off and on. Like all the rest, he was just a mutt, but I loved him, and we were inseparable for a time.

In my dream, Babe was lying on the ground, covered from muzzle to tail in ticks. Unable to get up, he was desperately sick. I knew he was going to die, and I felt helpless. Then it came to me: pray for him! In my dream, I got on my knees and began to pray. A bright, warm light that almost blinded me pierced the darkness around me. I felt happy and safe. It lasted for about only thirty seconds, but I wanted it to go on forever. When I turned back to Babe, he looked younger and healthier, like a puppy, tick-free. He was jumping around and playing, his fur shiny and healthy.

"Thank you, God," I said.

To my surprise, a deep, strong voice replied. "No, thank you."

THOUGH I WOULDN'T HAVE CONSIDERED MYSELF RELIGIOUS IN ANY WAY, I HAD SOME EXPERIENCES THAT I KNEW WERE OTHERWORLDLY IN ADDITION TO THOSE ENCOUNTERS WITH THAT LARGE FIGURE IN MY BEDROOM.

I woke up, slightly baffled by what I had dreamed but so sure it had some meaning I didn't understand. Though it made a deep impression, I didn't know what to do with this experience. I mentioned it to Mom the next day, but she didn't really understand either. "That's cool," she told me. I didn't have a priest or a pastor I could turn to for help, so I just tucked it away as a memory.

The next episode was about a year later and even stranger. In this dream, I was in my junior high school cafeteria. It was a typical lunchtime—crowded, noisy, kids pushing and shoving.

I recognized the faces of some of my classmates and friends. And then I saw Jesus walking through the cafeteria. I knew it was Him from some of the pictures I had seen on my occasional visits to church—He was bearded, wearing a robe and sandals. I had the same kind of peaceful feeling I remembered from my previous dream. The craziest part of it all was that everyone around was either ignoring Him or getting onto Him, pushing Him, and telling Him to get out of the way. After a while, Jesus turned and started to leave. He looked at me sadly, and I saw a tear running down His face.

I turned to my friends. "Guys," I said, "did you not know who that was? That was Jesus." They looked at me and shrugged as if to say, "So what?" and then I woke up, once again certain this was no ordinary dream but unclear as to its meaning.

There was a similar passage of time between this and my next dream. On this occasion, I found myself floating over a beautiful city that I just knew was heaven. The beautiful buildings and the streets were all lined with gold, while angelic voices and melodic harp sounds swirled around me. It was nowhere I had ever seen before in my life, and at the same time, it seemed completely familiar. It was where I knew I belonged and never wanted to leave. It was home.

My visit didn't last long. After a short time, I awoke, disappointed it was over. Once again, I told Mom what I had experienced, and this time, I was surprised by her response. "It's some kind of blessing that you're getting these dreams, Jackie Wayne," she told me. "Maybe you need to start writing them down so you don't forget them."

I thought that was a great idea. I got a journal and jotted down what I could remember of the dreams I'd had so far. Over the years, I would go on to fill two journals with different spiritual dreams, some of which I believe God used to encourage other people like He did when He gave Joseph dreams back in the Old Testament.

At the time, though, I wrote them down and put them away. Those experiences would linger with me for a few days, but I didn't know what to do with them. I thought that if I told my friends about them, they'd dismiss me as crazy, so I kept things to myself. Filed away but not entirely forgotten.

If we are assigned guardian angels to watch over us, as some people believe, I certainly kept mine busy. I suspect they may have had to tag team so they could get a break once in a while. In addition to the interference they seem to have run on keeping me safe from potential predators, I also walked away unscathed from two accidents that could easily have killed me.

I was in sixth grade when Royce's boss sold him a Lincoln he no longer wanted. With its roomy, dark brown leather interior and electric windows, it was the fanciest vehicle we'd ever had. In fact, it was the fanciest car in the whole neighborhood. For once, people weren't looking down on us but looking enviously. The first weekend we had it, Mom decided it would be fun to go on a little trip together. Jack was back staying with us at the time, so he piled in the rear seat with Tracy and me, Mom and Royce up front, and we set off to go get some purple hull peas from a pick-your-own farm out in the countryside.

As he waited to turn left across a major highway into the farm entrance, Royce flicked the latest of his chain-smoked

Pall Malls out of the driver's window. The next thing we knew, our world seemed to explode. A guy driving a big, heavy, flatbed truck behind us wasn't paying attention and didn't notice we had stopped until it was too late. The police later estimated he must have hit us rear-on at about 55 mph. The Lincoln flipped a couple of times before landing upright.

> **IF WE ARE ASSIGNED GUARDIAN ANGELS TO WATCH OVER US, AS SOME PEOPLE BELIEVE, I CERTAINLY KEPT MINE BUSY.**

Thankfully, they built those cars sturdy. None of us were wearing seat belts, so somehow, Mom ended up in the back with us. Tracy was slammed down on the floor. She, Jack, and I had all been drinking Cokes, but remarkably, none of the glass bottles had shattered when they flew out of our hands. The impact must have fractured the gas tank somehow because we were all soaked in fuel. Just as well Royce had finished that cigarette a few moments earlier.

We clambered out and stood at the side of the road, surveying our totaled vehicle. Amazingly, we all walked away without a scratch. One of the ambulance crew who came to the scene said that was probably because we literally hadn't known what hit us—we didn't have a chance to tense up in anticipation.

A WHOLE LIFE

We called Cheryl to come and drive us home. All I could think about was my birthday bicycle and my brand-new jean jacket and how we could never seem to hold onto anything nice and good for any length of time.

In my junior year, I got to go back to Dallas to spend a few days with my Scott. He was a year ahead of me and had just been bought a graduation gift by his mom a few weeks earlier—a sweet new silver and black Toyota Corolla with a sunroof and a stick shift. One night, he was going out with his girlfriend in her car and told me I could borrow his, if I liked. Did I ever.

I went over to Aunt Alice's home to pick up cousin Bubba and his girlfriend, Regina, who would later become his wife. We didn't have any plans other than to cruise around in this nice ride and see what the evening might bring. Bubba had some pot, and we stopped by a liquor store to buy a six-pack of beer. I still held to my pledge of not going to school buzzed, but I was cool with driving when I was stoned or drunk (make sense of that, if you can).

All three of us were up front, Regina sitting on Bubba's lap. None of us had our seat belts on. We'd been stooging around for quite some time, and I was pretty mellow by this point. Coming down a side street to an intersection with a busy main road, I failed to notice the yield sign and sailed straight through—at least, partway. We were tee-boned by a young guy in his mom's Cadillac coming from our right at about 50 mph.

Our Toyota flipped three or four times, landing on its roof. We bounced around inside like loose change in a washing machine, but somehow, we all crawled out uninjured. Again, maybe literally not knowing what hit us was a kind of protection.

Somehow, we not only escaped getting hurt but also managed to avoid getting into trouble. We must have smelled of weed, and there were beer cans in the vehicle, but when the police arrived, either they didn't notice, or they chose not to. They didn't require a sobriety test of me. I didn't even get a ticket, even though I admitted I hadn't seen the road sign. Relieved, my bigger concern now was how I was going to tell Scott I had wrecked his new car.

I called his home from a nearby convenience store, and before too long, he and his mom arrived at the scene. Scott looked at his crumpled Toyota and then at me. "Wow," he said, "you did a great job on that." He even took a picture of me standing by the wreck, grinning. Scott's mom was equally gracious. She hugged me and said, "I'm so glad you are all okay. We have insurance. The car can be replaced, but you can't."

Their super-cool response wasn't just in the heat of the moment, either. Neither of them ever subsequently mentioned what had happened in a negative way, another testimony to their great kindness to me.

I'd like to be able to say that all these instances of some kind of a caring hand over me were a signpost to me, pointing the way. But the truth is, I didn't see them that clearly. They were more like a background thread woven through the chaos, hinting that there was more to life than what I was experiencing. Only later would I be able to look back and gratefully trace that constant presence.

CHAPTER 13

Most storm clouds have a silver lining; it can just take time to recognize them. Moving from Dallas to small-town Louisiana as a fifteen-year-old was disruptive in many ways, but my time there also sowed some seeds that would bear fruit later in my life.

In addition to discovering I had a gift for connecting with people from a stage, I learned the satisfaction of hard work. I'd had jobs back in Dallas, but there's a world of difference between stacking shelves in an air-conditioned store and stacking hay in a barn where it's 120 degrees.

On first arriving in Quitman, I did what I was used to—I worked at a convenience store and washed dishes at a restaurant. Then I joined some of the guys hauling hay in the summertime. It was eye-opening: at first, the physical exertion and the heat wiped me out. But I found that I loved going home bone-tired at the end of the day, feeling like I had really earned every cent. It gave me even greater satisfaction in what I was able to do with the money.

As well as helping Tracy out here and there and buying my own clothes, I saved for a car. While nearly all the other juniors and seniors had their own vehicles, I was still stuck having to take the bus if I couldn't get a ride from a friend, who I'd slip a few bucks to help with the gas. Finally, in my senior year, I managed to sock away $500. Scouring the ads, I found a red Ford Mustang II for sale about thirty miles away. Mom drove me over, and I handed over my money. It wasn't a great car, but it was my very own. I no longer had to rely on other people, which meant up to that point, I had been restricted to double-dating unless the girl had a car of her own, and being driven around by a girl wasn't too cool. Plus, my new ride had a nice, roomy back seat.

Between working and partying, school wasn't high on my agenda in my senior year. I turned up dutifully and still always sober, but I didn't put in a lot of effort while I was there. Some of the teachers tried to encourage me by saying I had potential if I put my mind to things, but it didn't inspire me to change, other than for the effort I put into the senior play. Somehow, though, I did enough to scrape by, becoming the first guy in my family's history to graduate high school.

With vague plans to give college a shot, I took an interim summer job with the city as a garbageman. Most people looked down on trash collecting, but for me, there was something about the physical exertion and not caring what people thought that attracted me. That decision gave me an invaluable short apprenticeship with Mr. Zeno.

A genial old Black guy who also pastored a small church in town, he had been working as a garbageman for forty years. "I'm doing this so my kids can have better," he told me. Mr. Zeno was proud that both of his children had gone on to college, one to study law and the other to pursue a career in education.

They did trash a little differently in Quitman. We didn't collect it from outside people's homes, like back in Dallas. Residents took their refuse to big dumpsters located around town, which then had to be emptied. Because people weren't leaving their trash outside their own places, they could be a little less careful about how they deposited it. Some would be scattered around the dumpster, which I would have to gather up before climbing on top of the pile and stomping it down so we could load it onto our truck and take it to the central dump to be emptied.

In addition to the usual domestic trash, I'd have to deal with the hazards of country life—dog carcasses and leftovers from hunters who had cleaned deer before putting them in their freezers. It wasn't uncommon that I'd be crawling with flies and maggots. All of this in temperatures topping 100 degrees.

While I was out there getting sweaty and stinky, Mr. Zeno was sitting in the air-conditioned cab, acting as supervisor. I didn't begrudge him that; he'd earned it. Actually, I don't believe he was taking advantage of me. I think he was helping me build some character.

We'd chat as we drove around. He'd tell me something about what he had preached on the weekend. I'd tell him that I had been out partying with friends without going into too much detail. "Just remember, Jackie, those girls are God's daughters," he would say gently. I never felt like I was being lectured or looked down on, though I didn't take his admonitions to heart.

There were a couple of other benefits to the garbage gig. It was weekdays only, leaving evenings and weekends free for me to have fun. Getting home at the end of the day, I'd strip off and wash in an outside shower Mom had rigged up because she didn't want me in the house smelling as I did.

A WHOLE LIFE

With no examples of people who had pursued a career path in my family, my plans for the future were vague, to say the least. I decided to give college a try because my teachers thought it would be a good idea, and I chose Louisiana State University (LSU) because it seemed to be the cheapest option.

Having to declare a major, I decided on geology. This wasn't a well-thought-out decision: I'd never had any interest in the subject, but since living in Louisiana, I had observed that any people I knew with money were somehow involved in the oil business. One of the girls I had dated lived in the nicest house I had ever seen, complete with a swimming pool, and her father was an oil field geologist.

Given that I wasn't seriously interested in what I had gone to college to study, it's not surprising that things didn't turn out too well. My lack of focus was exacerbated by the sweet housing situation I had landed in. My friend David Schmidt had also opted for LSU, and he had a single aunt in Baton Rouge who had a nice home and let us room there. This was back before colleges required freshmen to live on campus to get acclimated to life as a single young adult away from parental supervision. With no one watching over me, I spent more time on Bourbon Street in New Orleans, an hour and a quarter's drive away, than I did in school.

I stuck to my rule about not going to classes high or hungover, but there was a shift in how I applied the rule. It no longer meant I'd be forward-thinking and ensure I didn't get into a scene that might leave me incapacitated the next day. It meant if I woke up hungover, I just didn't go to class.

Heightening my disinterest was the fact that I'd gotten a part-time job at the mall as a runner for JCPenney. That helped pay for my partying, and I had met someone to do it with, a high school senior I bumped into at the mall with a bit of a wild side to her.

When the management at Penney's took a shine to me and offered me a full-time position it seemed to be the path of least resistance. College just never clicked with me, somehow—though, to be fair, I hadn't given it a good shot, of course. When my first report cards came with "incompletes," that was enough. I never formally withdrew; I simply never set foot on campus again.

For the time being, having plenty of money in my pocket and someone to spend it on and with was enough. But gradually, I began to realize that while I may not have a plan for my life, I needed a sense of direction because just going around in circles gets old after a while. This was probably the longest I'd dated any girl, and I was recognizing that sex alone wasn't enough of a glue to keep us together; we broke up. Finally, after about six months, I woke up one day and realized that Baton Rouge wasn't where I was supposed to be.

> **I BEGAN TO REALIZE THAT WHILE I MAY NOT HAVE A PLAN FOR MY LIFE, I NEEDED A SENSE OF DIRECTION BECAUSE JUST GOING AROUND IN CIRCLES GETS OLD AFTER A WHILE.**

Being back in Quitman only further emphasized how adrift I was. My old high school friends who had gone on to different colleges were doing well, by all accounts. Those who had stayed home and followed the family line to the paper mill seemed content with their lot.

I revisited something I had briefly considered before going to LSU: joining the services. Jack had gone into the army and seemed to be doing okay, so I called him to ask what he thought. "Well, Jackie Wayne, I don't mean to be rude, but I don't think you'd survive boot camp," he told me. "You're not built for it. I've heard that the Air Force is more like a country club; maybe you should give them a try."

Jack wasn't far off the mark. At the Air Force recruiting office, they told me that I was borderline for acceptance because I was too skinny. At 5 ft 11 in, I weighed just 125 pounds, not because I didn't eat but because my metabolism just burned off whatever I consumed. They okayed my application and told me to go home and try to bulk up some before I reported for training in a few weeks. Instead, I spent the time partying.

My first time on a plane, flying from Shreveport, Louisiana, to Lackland Air Force Base in San Antonio, Texas, was fun. But after that, it all went downhill rapidly. Clearly, I hadn't really thought through what I had signed up for. Having spent most of my recent time doing what I wanted when I wanted, I now had people telling me what to do in no uncertain terms. I lay on my bunk that first night thinking, *This is awful. I have screwed up big-time.*

Things only got worse the next day. My hair was shaved, I was given a bunch of shots, and I had to trade my contact lenses for the standard-issue black-rimmed spectacles known as birth control glasses for their dorky look. And so it went. I wasn't lazy—I liked the reward of hard work—but I just couldn't get the hang of this new regime. My uniform was never fixed quite right; my bed was never made quite right. I was constantly getting yelled at.

About a month in, I was sitting with a guy I'd befriended and lamenting. "I just don't belong here, but I don't know how to get out," I told him. "And I've signed up for four years...."

He told me how he'd heard someone had jumped out of a window a few weeks earlier and killed himself. As a result, all the chiefs were on high alert because they didn't want something like that to happen again. "I've been told that if you go and tell the sergeant you're suicidal, they won't want you around."

While I was unhappy, I wasn't thinking of killing myself, but I figured I might as well try playing that card. I went to my drill sergeant and told him I was having suicidal thoughts. Almost before I knew it, I was being interviewed first by a counselor and then by a psychologist. I must have managed to present a convincing case because soon after, I was told that I was being discharged.

After two weeks in a sort of halfway house, while they processed all the necessary paperwork, I was back in Quitman again with no job and no idea what I was going to do.

I was feeling like a failure. I may not have achieved much by other people's standards up to this point, but I had prided myself on at least being able to take care of myself. I'd never been a quitter. Now, here I was, having dropped out of school and the military with nothing to look forward to; job prospects in Quitman were slim. I didn't even have a car, having sold it before going to San Antonio.

Help came from an unexpected source. Scott and I had kept in touch from time to time after I'd left Dallas, and I told him about my situation on one of our calls. He told me how things were going well for him: he'd gotten a good job in the produce department of a high-end grocery store in a nice part of Dallas, and he was settled in his own apartment. In fact, he went on, he was looking for a roommate and his employer was looking for more staff. Why didn't I join him, he said? We could even carpool to work until I saved up enough to buy my own wheels.

I MAY NOT HAVE ACHIEVED MUCH BY OTHER PEOPLE'S STANDARDS UP TO THIS POINT, BUT I HAD PRIDED MYSELF ON AT LEAST BEING ABLE TO TAKE CARE OF MYSELF. I'D NEVER BEEN A QUITTER.

Done. I used the last of my money to buy a Greyhound ticket to return to Dallas and reconnect with my old friend. In short order, I had a job in the produce department of a grocery store, and I was at the top of my game. At one stage, I was dating four checkout girls, without any of them knowing about the others. Sometimes, I'd been working on one of the displays and look over to the registers and wink, with two or three of the cashiers winking back at me.

Cheryl, who was living in Dallas at the time, had kindly co-signed on a car loan for me, so I had transportation, plus a nice apartment, plenty of pot and alcohol, and all the sex I could dream of. Life should have been perfect by all measures. But the empty hole I'd been trying to paper over kept getting wider and deeper. I tried to drown out this nagging sense of something missing by doubling down, kind of like turning the radio up in your car to mask that ominous knocking sound from the engine.

Having moved out of Scott's into a place of my own because I and his live-in girlfriend didn't get along too well, I fell into a depression. Many evenings, I would sit alone in the dark, smoking weed and listening to Pink Floyd. One night, this thought stabbed through the fog: *Why don't you just kill yourself? That will solve the emptiness.*

This shook me. I'd known several family members commit suicide—Garry and cousin William among them. William had never gotten over the crash in which Bobby Joe died. Relatives said he blamed himself. I'd shaken my head when I heard about William's death, unable to fathom how anyone could take their own life. And now, here I was contemplating the same thing. I was scared.

The only person I could think to call was Mom. I told her what had been going through my mind and about the second thing I'd heard in my head: that I needed to go back to Louisiana, which I really didn't want to do.

"You need some help," she said. "And maybe you should come back home." She and Royce drove to Dallas, loaded me and my stuff in their pickup truck, and took me back to Louisiana.

The darkness didn't lift entirely, but it decreased some. I got a job in the produce department of a grocery store again and soon got offered the chance to become the department manager at a new location opening soon in Shreveport. Things were looking up a bit. As my sense of heaviness eased, I drifted back into my familiar ways, reconnecting with some girls I had known back in high school. More sex and drugs and rock-n-roll.

CHAPTER 14

My life changed the day after a blowout Friday night party at a well-to-do friend's mansion. His folks were out of town, and we invited some girls over. There was video porn playing on the television, lots of drinking and drugs, and freewheeling sex. All a young man could wish for, right?

Well, somewhere in the early hours, I suddenly decided that I'd had enough. Or, more accurately, too much. Remember those times as a kid when you had just one more spoonful of your favorite ice cream, but it tipped you over the edge—you went from ravenous to nauseous? Something inside me said that I needed to go home.

I really shouldn't have driven because I was pretty drunk and high, but I simply couldn't stay there another moment despite the protests of the other partyers. I made the thirty-minute trip cautiously, flopped onto my bed, and lay there, unable to sleep. My head wasn't spinning, but my heart was.

After finally drifting off to sleep, I was awoken by a knocking at the front door. Mom and Royce were away for the weekend, and Tracy was out somewhere, so there was no one else around to answer. For some reason, I decided to go see who it was.

Moving slowly, feeling pretty hungover, I opened the door in my rumpled T-shirt and shorts. Two young women were standing there, dressed simply and plainly in white shirts with straight, mid-length skirts. One of them in particular was quite cute. She spoke with a South African accent, which only added to her appeal. They told me they were from a church, and they were visiting homes in the area. They would love to come in and tell me about their Savior, Jesus, they said.

This was not how I'd thought my Saturday morning would go, but I told them, "Err, sure, but not real loud, okay, because I'm a bit hungover right now."

They laughed, then one of them asked if anyone else was at home. When I told them no, they looked at each other questioningly. "We're not really supposed to be alone in a house with a single man," one of them explained.

"That's fine," I said, moving to close the door.

But before I could, the South African speaker said that she thought it would be fine for them to come in together, so they did.

We sat in the family room for an hour that seemed to fly by. They started by telling me something about their church, and then they gave me a leaflet that they said would explain the atonement for me—how Jesus died for our sins.

My initial attraction to my South African visitor gave way to interest and curiosity. What would they think if they knew what I had been up to just a few hours earlier? We talked and talked, and I was intrigued by the idea that I could be forgiven for what I'd done wrong, especially given the fact that I was sitting in the groggy aftermath of a night of debauchery. Surely what they were talking about couldn't apply to me—I was far too wayward?

As the conversation drew to a close, one of the young women said they wanted to leave me with some homework. "We're not asking you to pray about whether our religion is right or wrong," she said. "That's not why we're here today. But I see something in your eyes that tells me some of this is resonating with you. So, I want to ask you to do this: after we've gone, will you get on your knees and pray about what we have said about Jesus and His forgiveness, and see if you believe what we are saying is true?"

I told them I would but, truthfully, once I had closed the door behind them, I dismissed the request. It all sounded so far-fetched. Sure, what they had said had been interesting, but it really couldn't apply to me.

I shuffled around the house for the next couple or so hours as my hangover eased, a little voice in my head repeating, *Read that pamphlet. Read that pamphlet.*

Finally, sometime mid-afternoon, I picked it up and read. It explained how through His death on the cross and resurrection, Jesus had paid the price for us to overcome sin, adversity, and death.

I didn't fall to my knees so much as feel myself being pressed down there by an unseen force. Not in an overbearing, oppressive way but almost kindly. I decided to pray as I had been asked to: "Lord, please forgive me. I want to know who You are." I was sincere, but the words felt a bit awkward.

If you have ever had an IV inserted for some kind of infusion, you will have a sense of what I experienced next. Starting at my toes and then rolling up through my legs, into my torso, out along my arms, and up out of the top of my head, came a warm glow. Then, I heard a voice, audibly as best I remember: "You are forgiven. Go and do My work."

This was all so unexpected, to say the least. I lay on the floor for a while, not wanting or daring to move. I wasn't quite sure of all that had just happened, but I knew that I'd had an encounter with . . . God. When I finally stood up, I felt like I did after I'd come home from a day hauling garbage with Mr. Zeno and taken a long, hot shower—clean, free from the funky cloud of decay that hung around me.

When I'd left the party the previous night, I'd said I'd be back on Saturday evening, but I was a no-show. I simply had no desire to be in that kind of environment—but I had an insatiable desire to understand more of what was going on. I dug out an old Bible Mom had tucked away on a shelf somewhere and spent the whole night reading it. I was fascinated and thrilled, drinking it in like a cold glass of water after a hot day in the sun.

Next morning, I tidied myself up and went to the church my visitors had told me about. I'm not sure who was more surprised to see me there—them or me. I told them a little about what had happened to me after they had left, and they were thrilled and possibly just a little surprised. They told me this Sunday of the month was one in which members of the church got to stand up and tell about what God may have been doing in their lives, rather than hearing a regular sermon. Would I like to take part?

My two immediate reactions were yes and no. Yes because, unlikely as it sounds, I really wanted to tell people what had happened. It was so real and remarkable I felt like I had to let it out; that if I didn't, I might burst. No because, with all I had done wrong, did I have the right to speak about such things?

Eventually, I decided I just had to contribute. I went down to the front of the church and introduced myself and told a little about what I had experienced. Surprisingly, I found that I wasn't nervous. In fact, I felt quite at ease and at home. *This is even better than being in a play*, I thought, remembering my high school performance. Afterward, the two visiting sisters came up and gave me a demure hug and several people shook my hand and thanked me, saying I had touched them.

The next week was like I was in some kind of a cocoon. I went to work, but then I'd come straight home and start reading the Bible again. It was unreal: the guy who just a week or so ago couldn't stop thinking about sex now only had the scriptures on his mind. I couldn't sleep—I got through the Bible from cover to cover by the next weekend. It felt like it was alive, a personal message from heaven to me. Friends called and left messages wanting to know where I was and what was up, but I just ignored them.

Back at church the following weekend, the service was about missionary work. A young woman spoke about how she had just returned from a two-year mission to another part of the country to tell people about God, and how much she had grown as a result. The next speaker also talked about mission work. Then, in the Sunday school class that followed, someone talked about preparing to go on a church mission. *I want to do that*, I thought. I knew that most of the other young people who went on these missions were a couple of years younger than me, so I felt like I had no time to waste. After the church service, I was invited home for lunch by a couple, where I asked them more about what this mission thing involved. "How soon can I go on one?" I asked. I knew I had to be about God's work—whatever that meant.

> **IT WAS UNREAL: THE GUY WHO JUST A WEEK OR SO AGO COULDN'T STOP THINKING ABOUT SEX NOW ONLY HAD THE SCRIPTURES ON HIS MIND.**

They explained the system: first, I'd need to be baptized and then I would have to complete a series of six studies and have an interview with the local bishop. "When can we start the studies?" I asked. We spent four hours going through the first two lessons that night.

Though I had been told that new members of the church usually didn't get approved for a mission until they had been around for at least a year, I knew that I couldn't wait that long. I had to get out there as soon as possible.

When I met with the bishop, I told him my story, going into enough detail to be honest without making his hair curl in horror. He listened carefully. "You know, young man, we normally don't just let somebody join the church and go off on a mission straight away," he said. "But the Lord just witnessed to me that you are supposed to go. So, let's try to get this done!"

The bishop outlined some steps I would need to complete. He was sure I was sincere, he said, but given the gravity of some of the things I had told him, I would need to meet with a more senior church leader when they were visiting the area.

From some research I'd done, I knew that the person I had to see was a well-respected authority. I was nervous all week. When I walked into our meeting, he greeted me warmly, a sheet of paper on the desk in front of him. Then he surprised me.

"Young man," he said, "I had all these questions to ask you, but when you came into the room, I got a witness from God that you have been forgiven, so who am I to judge you? I don't need to know anything more: I approve of you going on a mission. In fact, we can start the paperwork today, if you would like."

A lot can happen in a month: I'd quit the party scene, joined a church, and been approved to go on a two-year mission. Every day I checked the mailbox as eagerly as Tracy and I looked for the welfare check, waiting to learn where I would be going. Finally, the news arrived: Wyoming and Montana. For someone who had only ever been to two states, both in the South, it sounded very exotic.

There were several weeks before I was due to go to a training camp prior to heading north. I'd been offered a promotion at another store in the grocery store chain I was working at, with a sizable pay increase, but I turned it down. "We can give you more money," I was told. I explained it wasn't about the pay; I had something else I had to do. Then I quit my existing job, and I spent hours every day reading the Bible. I felt like I had so much time to make up for that I couldn't waste a moment. I tried to explain to Mom a little of what was going on, but she didn't really understand. She and Royce were still having their squabbles, but I was somehow protected from it all, in this bubble of peace and anticipation.

A WHOLE LIFE

I felt I should fast, something people at church had spoken about. I'd heard about religious people going without food and even water for periods to heighten their spiritual experiences but that all sounded a bit weird to me. I'd gone hungry plenty of times before, but never by choice, and I'd just been miserable. But the prodding was undeniable. So, I deliberately went without food or water for three full days, and I was amazed. During that time, I spent countless hours reading the Bible and it seemed to come even more alive. It felt like all my senses were heightened.

One story in particular stuck out to me—the account of Saul's conversion on the road to Damascus. There he was, one of the fiercest persecutors of the early church, complicit in the deaths of some of those early believers, when Jesus appeared to him as a blinding white light, causing him to fall to the ground. Rising, Paul, as he became known, would commit his life to serving Jesus and become one of the greatest figures in Christian history. This account inspired me: if God could take someone as wayward as Paul and use him to extend God's kingdom, there was hope for me. I may not have persecuted people for their beliefs like Paul, but I had lived far from how God wanted.

Some old friends came over to the house to ask after me. I didn't feel ready to talk a lot about what had happened, so I just said I was focused on some other things right then. When I finally told them about my mission shortly before I left, one of them was astonished: "Jack Jameson's not going to touch a girl for two years? I don't believe it."

I won't pretend that I didn't notice pretty girls anymore; I did. Only now I wasn't looking at them as just a conquest, someone to use for my personal pleasure. I felt like a hole inside of me was healing up, as if it had been gently stitched together. All the sex and drugs and rock-n-roll had never really satisfied me, but this new sense of meaning and purpose did.

Though I knew I had been forgiven, some of my past actions weighed on me a little. In particular, I felt bad for the way I had mistreated so many girls. I don't mean physically but emotionally—I'd used them for sex in an attempt to fill that big gap inside of me. I called a few of them to try to apologize. A couple of them blew me off, telling me I was dumb: maybe what I'd said had made them feel bad about themselves and they didn't like it. They hung up on me. One girl was kind, though—she cried and thanked me for telling her I was sorry.

> **I FELT LIKE A HOLE INSIDE OF ME WAS HEALING UP, AS IF IT HAD BEEN GENTLY STITCHED TOGETHER.**

Having quit my job, my finances were low, so I sold my car to help pay for my mission expenses. Thankfully, the church I had joined stepped up to help with the rest of the money I needed. I'd be living on $300 a month for the next two years.

After three weeks at a missionary training center, I boarded a little prop plane with half a dozen or so other young people, heading to Billings, Montana. It was the middle of winter, the wind blowing that small aircraft almost sideways. All I could think was, *I'm going to die before I even get there!*

CHAPTER 15

Landing safely none too soon for me in Billings, I then realized I was in more danger of freezing to death. The pilot announced it was two degrees outside, with a wind chill factor of ten below. I had two suits and a pair of dress shoes but no coat.

Welcomed by the local church leaders, we were taken to dinner and told where our first assignments would be. After we'd finished eating, the head guy announced that we were going out door-to-door visiting right then. Talk about jumping into the deep end. I was surprised.

"Aren't we going to wait until it warms up a bit to do that?" I asked.

"No, son," I was told. "We'll be waiting till June for that to happen!"

Braced against the biting wind, we were driven to a trailer park on the side of town where I was paired up with another young missionary who had already been in the area for a while. It was so cold I thought I was getting frostbite. After a few fruitless calls, an old guy opened the door to his trailer and invited us in. There was a potbelly stove in the middle of his living room, and I went over, sat down, and took my shoes off so I could rest my icy feet on the stove. My companion looked a bit surprised, but our host told him, "That's fine; it sure is cold out there."

The next day, my new partner took me down to the local Army Navy store so I could pick out a pair of Sorel boots, a heavy dress coat and thick gloves, one of those Russian hats with ear flaps, and long johns.

And so began what would become the two most pivotal and foundational years of my life, the equivalent of a four-year degree. To this day, much of what I discovered and learned while I was there shapes my life. I say you couldn't give me a million dollars to take back that experience—and you couldn't pay me a million dollars to go and do it again! In many ways, I went to Montana as a boy, and I returned as a man.

The first lesson was discipline. This assignment was not for the faint-hearted. It was serious business. The church ran its outreaches with a military-like efficiency and expected us to follow orders. We were paired off with another missionary with whom we roomed for a few weeks before moving on somewhere else and making a new partner.

The day started at 5:30 a.m. with ninety minutes of personal study. Then it was breakfast and out on visitation, either knocking on doors and hoping we might get invited in or following up on appointments that may have been made for us to go around and have a discussion with someone. This would keep us busy anywhere from four to eight hours a day, Tuesday through Saturday. Sundays we were expected to be in church, of course, and Mondays were our personal day to take care of things like laundry and writing letters home, as we were encouraged to do.

While I was enthusiastic and sincere about what I was doing, I soon realized that we were essentially "selling faith," if you will. We had something we wanted other people to be interested in. So, the same rules that applied to the retail world applied to the religious world. For instance, a warm lead is always much better than a cold call.

Not everyone appreciated our appearance at their door. At one house in Butte, the owner came to the door with a shotgun and told us he was not interested. "You have thirty seconds to get off my porch and five minutes to get off my property or I'm going to shoot you dead!" My partner and I took off running, and as we hurried away the guy fired over our heads. I just about wet my pants.

At another home, the old lady came to the door and when we explained why we were there she said for us to wait just a minute. Then she returned holding a pan of boiling water which she threw at us. I managed to escape with a lightly burned ankle.

There was also the occasion when a woman opened the door holding a leashed Doberman Pinscher that she set on me. It lunged at my crotch, but thankfully, the pants I was wearing were a little oversized and baggy, so the attack required only sewing, not surgery.

Scary as they were, those kinds of responses were by far the exception. Many people were surprisingly kind to two young men in suits arriving unannounced at their front door.

I quickly learned that you needed to establish some kind of connection before you got down to business. As we walked up to the door, I would look out for something I could make a remark about. Maybe there were pretty flowers in the yard, which I would tell them reminded me of home (okay, there may have been a bit of embellishment there). Or I would comment on the cool car parked in the driveway; just like one I'd always wanted, I would say.

Then you needed to ask them a question or two to get them talking about themselves: after all, most of us are our favorite subjects. How did they grow those roses? Was that the 454 model, like my brother had? Only then was it time to get around to introducing ourselves and explaining we'd like to talk to them about God. By the time we were inside, we were more like friends than strangers. Some of the barriers were already lowered.

I learned to read people's body language. If they smiled when they opened the door, chances were they were going to be more approachable—certainly more so than if they had their arms folded. Surprisingly, I discovered that going door to door when it was cold could be beneficial. Sure, some people chose not to answer when we knocked but those that did typically felt sorry for us, especially if we shivered a little, and they would welcome us in. It also turned out that arriving around dinnertime could be advantageous on occasions; we'd get invited in to have something to eat with them.

Saturdays were good for canvassing, too. Oftentimes, someone would be out in the yard doing chores and it was easy to say hi and get into a conversation. Some folks would brush us off because they were busy, but others were glad for the excuse to stop and chat a while.

When I had first arrived in Montana, I had been concerned that my strong Southern accent might make people look at me oddly, but when I saw that many warmed to it, I may have even amped it up a little. Look for unexpected opportunities and play to those unlikely strengths.

A WHOLE LIFE

We weren't the only team in town. There were missionaries from another church group doing similar work and I would always check to see if any of their people were out on the street we intended to canvas. If so, I'd suggest we go somewhere else because we didn't want to seem like we were bugging people. I also learned that this group had a secret way of marking homes they had visited, to let others on their team know they had been there—a small pencil mark by the front door. That was another indicator to maybe leave it a while and come back another day.

Much of what I did was intuitive, but I also learned some things from a book I picked up in a thrift store, one time. I'd heard about Dale Carnegie's classic *How to Win Friends and Influence People*[29] and found that it explained why some of the things I did worked in connecting with people and also gave me more insights into what made people tick.

One thing I took away was the importance of listening, especially if, like me, you were happy to talk. I realized I needed to pause sometimes and give people who might be less talkative a chance to respond—and while I did, concentrate on what they were saying rather than thinking about what I intended to say next. Too many times we miss important clues people give us because we are not really paying attention to what they are saying—it's all about what we want to say.

I wasn't looking to make a name for myself; all I was interested in was making an impact on people's lives the way I had been affected by those girls' visit. But as I threw myself into the mission, word soon started to get around among church

---

[29] Dale Carnegie, *How to Win Friends and Influence People: How to Stop Worrying and Stop Living* (New York, NY: Pocket Books, 1998).

leaders about what was happening. And I took advantage of the opportunity.

> **TOO MANY TIMES WE MISS IMPORTANT CLUES PEOPLE GIVE US BECAUSE WE ARE NOT REALLY PAYING ATTENTION TO WHAT THEY ARE SAYING—IT'S ALL ABOUT WHAT WE WANT TO SAY.**

Whenever we were moved on to a new area—which happened every couple of months, because church leaders didn't want us to get too comfortable in any one situation—the first thing I would do would be to go and introduce myself to the local bishop. I'd tell him briefly about my experience and ask if I might speak in his church the next Sunday morning.

Invariably, they were more than pleased to have me do so. Fact was, I was a little bit different than most of the missionaries out there. First, I was a little bit older, which can make a difference in your early twenties. Then there was my background. Most of the other members of the teams I was part of had grown up in the church and had not experienced life in the way I had. No criticism, there; in some ways I almost envied them. But for many of them, the mission was just part of what was expected of them on their journey to adulthood. It was more like an obligation than an opportunity. It seemed like many of them were marking time, going through the motions. And some were actively taking advantage of the opportunity of being away from home to push the boundaries; more than one young man got "terminated" for getting too friendly with some of the local young female church members.

There were exceptions to this lightweight involvement, to be sure. One of the guys I was partnered with for a time had grown up in the church but only recently gotten serious about his faith, as I was—so much so, in fact, that he had put a pause on his university studies, and a promising basketball career, to give two years to mission work. Then there was a guy who, in his mid-twenties, quit his job to go on a mission because of how he felt God had changed his life. That really impressed me.

Once I got to speak at a local church, I knew that things were going to be a bit easier in the weeks that followed. I'd typically be invited to homes by parents who hoped some of my zeal might rub off on their kids. I would generate introductions to some of their friends because I wasn't too "churchy." That meant less cold calling.

If I found myself with a Sunday evening or a Wednesday evening free, I would go to one of the other kinds of church in town. After all, a good salesperson knows what their competitors are offering, right? You can't have an informed conversation with someone if you don't know anything about their background. Next time I knocked on a door where someone told me they went to Such-and-Such Church, I could tell them I'd been there, and what friendly folks they were. Or maybe they had even seen me there. Again, I was overcoming a barrier to connection. I didn't slip into these churches dressed down so people wouldn't notice; I wore my "visitation" suit with my name badge on it. I wasn't trying to hide anything, and if people wanted to engage me in conversation thinking that they would "convert" me, that was fine by me as long as we got to talk.

These and my other strategies meant that pretty soon I was recording numbers of visits and people wanting to get baptized that got church leaders' attention. Some of them may have thought that my approach was a little unorthodox, but they couldn't deny the results. As a consequence, I was appointed a zone leader after just a couple of months in the field, which was almost unheard of. Especially for a newcomer to the church.

This role meant overseeing the other members of the team in my area and offering some coaching and encouragement. And the occasional kick in the pants, when it was appropriate. After a while, I had other missionaries requesting to get paired with me for a few weeks. Apart from anything else, I had a reputation for getting invited to meals! Fortunately, I have always had a healthy metabolism, otherwise I would have finished my time not just hopefully wiser but also a lot heavier. Sometimes the fridge back at our lodgings was so full of doggie bags we'd end up having to throw away lots of uneaten food.

One time, another missionary who had been teamed with me suddenly started recording a notable increase in the number of baptisms he was being asked to arrange. He was a nice enough guy, but he wasn't exactly a ball of fire, so I was intrigued by the development. What had made this sudden difference in his impact, I asked him?

"Well," he said a little sheepishly. "I've started telling your story."

Before I had time to be either offended or impressed, he went on to explain that he wasn't passing my experience off as his own. Rather, he said, he was telling people about someone he knew, because he knew the story to be true, not just an anecdote. And because it carried weight with and for him, it made an impact on others when he told them. Here was another lesson I learned: the power of story. It doesn't have to be yours to resonate with people, it's all about how you share it.

While it was encouraging to hear some of the ways I was having an impact on people, for me it was never about the numbers. Indeed, there were times when I'd actually downplay the church side of things. I was more interested in people wanting to know more about God, whatever that looked like for them, and whatever direction they took them in. Sure, I was happy to tell them about the church where I'd found a home, but I wasn't going to force that on anyone.

In some ways I was a bit of a maverick, but the church leaders rolled with it because they could see I was sincere, and they couldn't deny the results. Until I came to the end of my two years.

I'd spent time in some of the most beautiful parts of Montana, none more lovely than Missoula, out by Glacier National Park: when people talk about "God's country," that surely has to be in the running. I was happy when I was told that instead of moving on to a new situation again for the last two months, I could see out my time in Missoula.

And then I got word that I was actually going to have to finish my mission in Casper, Wyoming. No offense, but this was not what I was hoping for. The town was known for being the place some of the no-hoper missionaries got sent, because it already had a fairly strong church presence. They could sort of just coast by there. In addition, because of the numbers already there, a zone leader wasn't needed. I was effectively being demoted.

I was bummed. I'd worked hard at not letting the success I had enjoyed go to my head. Yes, it was nice to have people say good things about you, but I knew anything of value wasn't ultimately because of me, it was because God had chosen to use me. Still, I wasn't happy with this decision. I decided to appeal the decision to the mission president—surely this couldn't be right? When we spoke, he was almost apologetic, but firm. God had told him as clear as a bell that I was to go to Casper, he said, and he wasn't going to argue with God about that. Case closed.

> YES, IT WAS NICE TO HAVE PEOPLE SAY GOOD THINGS ABOUT YOU, BUT I KNEW ANYTHING OF VALUE WASN'T ULTIMATELY BECAUSE OF ME, IT WAS BECAUSE GOD HAD CHOSEN TO USE ME.

I was about as mad as I could ever remember being. For a couple of days, I stewed hard, grumbling to myself. But then I decided, did I want these two years to end on a sour note? I'd been disciplined and followed all the rules thus far; was I going to let my frustration spoil what had been such an enriching experience? I decided to suck it up and submit to directions.

It wasn't easy. Word started to get around that I must have done something wrong to have been effectively benched like this and, feeling I needed to remain loyal, I just had to bite my tongue and not say anything in my defense. As a group of us made the eight-hour drive down to Casper from Missoula, the others getting dropped off at their new appointments along the way, my mood became increasingly gray.

Determined to make the best of things, I went along to the local church my first Sunday there, as usual. At the close of the service, a kindly lady sitting in front of me turned around and asked if I was one of the new missionaries she had heard were coming. I told her yes, ma'am, and she said she had grown up in Florida. "I bet you miss having homemade Southern food," Mrs. Bertagnole said, inviting me for dinner the following Saturday evening. I went over and got to enjoy some really good fried chicken and met her husband, who had been out of town the previous weekend. He was equally welcoming, and I quickly warmed to him. He had been a long-time leader in the local church and had a spiritual depth to him that I admired. I began to visit him to talk about issues of faith.

A couple of weeks later, my missionary partner was invited over to the Bertagnoles' home for a Saturday evening meal with them and some of their ten children who were still at home. We were sitting chatting when the door opened and in came two young women, back from a run to the video store. Mrs.

Bertagnole introduced one of them as her daughter, Kim, back home for the weekend with her college roommate.

Suddenly, rather than a demotion, Casper seemed just about the greatest place on earth.

CHAPTER 16

Despite everything, I have to credit my mom with some of the success I experienced on my two-year mission and the positive qualities I sought to develop thereafter. She may not have set the greatest example in many ways when I was growing up, but I inherited some good traits from her.

She taught me not to put someone's kindness to a quality test. We were out fishing by the lake one day when a Black woman working the spot next to us brought a packet of cookies out of a bag. Turning to us, she asked me, "Hey, son, would you like one?"

>>>

SHE MAY NOT HAVE SET THE GREATEST EXAMPLE IN MANY WAYS WHEN I WAS GROWING UP, BUT I INHERITED SOME GOOD TRAITS FROM HER.

>>>

You might have thought cookies were a rare enough treat for me just to say thank you very much and take one, but for some reason, I asked, "What kind are they?" The next thing I knew, my head was ringing from the slap Mom had given me.

Later, she gave me a stern lecture. "Next time someone offers you food, you don't ask what kind. You just take it and eat it, you understand me?" she said. "I don't care if it's the worst-tasting thing in the world. You say, 'Thank you,' and you swallow it. You don't have to have seconds, but you never question it. You've been to bed hungry, Jackie Wayne, and so have I. When someone's being kind to you, it's rude to question them."

That lesson stuck with me and stood me in good stead during my few weeks in Riverton, Wyoming, while on my mission. Rumor had it that some folks in the poorer part of town ate dog, which made my mission partner nervous when we were invited for dinner at one of the homes there.

"There's no way I'm eating that," he told me.

"Listen," I said to him, echoing my mom, "whatever they serve us, we're going to say thank you, and we will eat it, okay? We're here on His work, so God will protect us!"

We never brought back a sample of what was put on our plates to be able to identify it definitively, but it was certainly unlike any meat I had ever eaten before. Gristly, gamy, awful-tasting—somehow, we managed to get it down without gagging. Having somehow cleared our plates, we were then offered seconds—which I was able to decline by telling our hosts that we'd had a late lunch that day, so we were still pretty full. On the way back to our lodgings, I was able to encourage my queasy-feeling partner by pointing out that a) we had survived and b) he had a great story to tell friends in the future.

On another occasion, I was visiting a little old lady with another mission partner. The woman must have been in her eighties and insisted on making us a ham and cheese sandwich. While she was out of the room, I swiveled around the jar of Miracle Whip she had used on our bread to read the label on the back: it had expired more than two years previously. That explained the green rather than yellow hue of the spread. Once again, we prayed hard and survived.

Though we never had very much, Mom would, from time to time, demonstrate unusual generosity. There was the day we were walking past someone collecting for The Salvation Army, and she looked in her purse. All she had was four dollars, but she insisted on donating a buck.

Aware that was one less chance I'd get a rare treat, I complained to her as we walked away. "Mom, you know we don't have much money ourselves," I whined. "Why would you give them some of what we had left like that?"

"Jackie Wayne," she said, "no matter how bad off we are, remember that there are always people doing worse than us."

Mom also taught me that there was no such thing as a stranger. We'd be down at the grocery store, and she would be looking at all the different cake mixes, so she would ask the woman standing nearby which one she'd recommend. Before you knew it, they would be standing there talking about like they were old friends for twenty minutes or more.

Though Mom's words and actions often seemed harsh and uncaring, she also had moments of kindness and concern. The encounter with the lady with the cookies while we were out fishing also illustrated Mom's attitude toward race. If she and the rest of the family held similar views about crime and immorality, they diverged when it came to color. Some of our relatives were pretty outspoken about their views on minorities—the N-word was used quite freely—but she never went along with that kind of talk.

Mom always taught us that you don't mistreat anyone because of the color of their skin. This was uncommon not only in our family but in the broader community at that time. The part of Dallas where we lived was pretty clearly divided into Black and White neighborhoods. While there may not have been a lot of outward, open hostility, there was a quiet undercurrent of prejudice and suspicion. That, in part, was why Fred at the Fireside Rec had made such an impression on me.

Mom never explained to me the reasons for her attitude, but I think it came from her personal experience. Growing up poor, she'd toiled alongside Black workers picking cotton with her family. They didn't just sweat together; they would eat together—some of their shared meals were where she'd learned to love things like collard greens. She seemed to realize that when you're bent over in the fields with bleeding hands, side by side, superficial differences fade away. You're more united in the struggles you share than by the difference of your skin. It was an attitude I observed and absorbed that shaped my life to this day.

Mom never showed much interest in politics or religion; they seemed like big topics way above everyday life. But she was a big fan of Ronald Reagan. We were watching him speak on television one time during his first term in office when she commented on how burdened he seemed by everything. So, she decided she was going to write him a letter.

In it, she told the president that she had voted for him in the last election and that she believed in him. She said that she had a son in the army—Jack, at the time—and she was proud that he could serve his country and his president.

A few weeks later, when I went out to collect the mail, there was an envelope from the White House. It was a personal letter to Mom from President Reagan. It wasn't one of those form thank-yous that go out, because it referred specifically to some of the things Mom had said in her letter. "Dear Evelyn," it began, thanking her for her support and her prayers and for her son's service.

As a big fan of President Reagan, too, I think I was more thrilled by her getting the letter than my mom was. She gave it to me many years later, and I had it examined, to discover a personal signature from him, not one of those duplicated ones. I have the letter framed, hanging in my office as both a reminder of a man and a leader I greatly admired and a woman who often confused and disappointed me but who could also demonstrate great thoughtfulness.

One of the things Mom prided herself on was never having bought her own drink in all her years going out to the bars. She would hang back and wait for some guy to come up and start sweet-talking her. And she could work a room; she would have made a fantastic salesperson if she had set her mind to it.

Once, when we were between cars, Mom decided to check out a local automobile sales listing even though she had just $27.50 saved toward a replacement vehicle. She loved Chevrolets and came across a 1960 model going for $1,500, one of those with the big rear fins. "Let's go check this out," she said to Uncle Ace, who was visiting. Though he told her it was a waste of time, she wouldn't take no for an answer, and he reluctantly gave in.

Sometime later, Mom drove Uncle Ace back to our place in her newly bought 1960 Chevrolet—for which she had paid a mere $27.50. "I don't believe it," he said, shaking his head. "I don't know all that your mom said, but she didn't stop talking for just about an hour and ended up getting that car for what she had. I've never seen anything like it in my life. I almost expected the owner to pay your mom to take it away from her!"

Mom may have scored an incredible bargain, getting her dream car for less than a fiftieth of the original asking price, but it didn't end there. Eight months or so later, Tracy and I went shopping with her at Menard's grocery store, and when we came out with our bags, a guy was standing by our car.

Drooling over our Chevrolet, he asked whether it was the one with a 350 engine in it. When Mom told him yes, he offered her $3,000 cash for it on the spot. "Done," she told him, and we had to call Aunt Alice from a pay phone to come and give us a ride home.

This ability to wheel and deal extended to other things. She could go to a garage sale and spin a tale about not having much money, load up our car to the roof with stuff for which she'd paid no more than $5 in total, then bring it home and resell it for a couple of hundred dollars.

Some of that bargain hunter gene has been passed on to me. To this day, some family members ask me to go with them when they are car shopping. I love the hunt, the challenge. Not that long ago, I went looking for a new Lincoln and found one stickered for $78,000. Four hours later, I drove it home, having paid $55,000. Thanks, Mom!

Whether it was cars, guys, or anything else, Mom didn't seem to want to hold on to anything too long. And not just what was hers. When I got home from my mission, I discovered she had sold all my belongings while I was away. Literally everything of mine was gone. There hadn't been much to leave stored in a cupboard when I left, but it was all meaningful. In addition to some clothes, there was my boom box and all my favorite cassettes, plus a few keepsakes from my childhood—including that *Planet of the Apes* play set my dad had bought me on our weekend together. I was so upset.

"Mom!" I cried in exasperation. "Where's all my stuff? What have you done with it?"

"I sold it," she said matter-of-factly. "You didn't need it."

Her actions probably shouldn't have surprised me as much as they did, in retrospect. I remembered that before I'd left on my mission trip, I'd come home one day to discover that my bed was outside in a yard sale with a pile of other things.

"What are you doing with my bed?"

"You're leaving, so you're not going to need it."

"Yeah, but I'm not going just yet. I'm still gonna be here for another couple more months."

"Whatever. You can sleep on the couch; it'll be fine."

I hadn't been expecting a hero's return when I got back to Louisiana, but I had hoped for some warmth after an absence of two years. Phone calls to family had been restricted to Mother's Day and Christmas because the mission leaders didn't want anyone getting too homesick, but I had dutifully written letters almost every week, as we were supposed to.

In them, I'd tell Mom what I had been up to and talk about some of the people I'd met, saying if someone reminded me of her. I tried not to sound too preachy, but I hoped she might pick up a bit about how my life had changed. In some of her rare letters back to me, Mom would say from time to time she was concerned about how things were going with Tracy, so I tried to plant some little seeds in my sister's life.

> **I HADN'T BEEN EXPECTING A HERO'S RETURN WHEN I GOT BACK TO LOUISIANA, BUT I HAD HOPED FOR SOME WARMTH AFTER AN ABSENCE OF TWO YEARS.**

Any thoughts that my absence had made Mom warmer were quickly evaporated. The morning after I returned, she came over to the couch where I was still lying after an uncomfortable night and began lecturing me on how I needed to get up, get going, and get a job. Did I think I could just laze around all day doing nothing?

I was discouraged, but I took some comfort from knowing that I wasn't the only person ever to have had a hard time being accepted at home. I remembered reading in the Bible how, after

Jesus began teaching and doing miracles, He went back to where He used to live, only for the people there to dismiss Him as just the local carpenter they'd always known Him as. I wasn't putting myself on par with the Son of God, but I figured if He, being perfect, was given a hard time, then I could surely expect something similar, given my background.

In some ways, being back home was like re-entry after being in space. No longer weightless, I was being pulled down by gravity. During those two years on my mission, I felt like I was in something of a sheltered environment, both because I was singularly focused on what I was doing and because I believed God had a measure of protection over me, kind of like a force field, as I was trying to serve Him. It felt like whatever was surrounding me lifted as soon as I walked back into the house.

Nonetheless, I tried to be a good example. I'd written quite often to Tracy when I was away, but she had responded only infrequently. I hoped some of our former closeness might be reawakened when I returned, but she didn't seem too interested. Whenever I tried to mention anything about what I'd been doing or God, she blew me off and told me not to lecture her.

Over the years, I had also been quite close to one of my nieces, who was not that much younger than me, by now in her mid-teens. While I was gone, she had gotten into some trouble that ended up with her being sent to some kind of detention center. I visited her there and tried to talk to her about God and tell her how my life had changed, but she wasn't having any of it. I wasn't trying to be judgmental, but that was how she seemed to take my concern. "Don't come here preaching at me, thinking you're better than me," she said. "I remember what you used to be like—the drinking, the drugs, the partying. You've got no business talking to me about what's right and wrong."

After the high of the past couple of years, it was all pretty discouraging. Having escaped chaos for a sense of purpose and meaning, it felt like I was in danger of sliding back into the same old disorder. I knew that I needed to exercise some of the discipline that had been required out on my mission if I was going to survive and thrive, only without the structure and environment that had been provided there. No one was going to come and bail me out. It was down to me to build a life based on the faith I'd discovered and the lessons I had learned about connecting with people and making a difference.

Fortunately, I had something to motivate me.

> **IT WAS DOWN TO ME TO BUILD A LIFE BASED ON THE FAITH I'D DISCOVERED AND THE LESSONS I HAD LEARNED ABOUT CONNECTING WITH PEOPLE AND MAKING A DIFFERENCE.**

CHAPTER 17

When I looked over at Kim, the young lady I was being introduced to at the Bertagnoles' home in Casper, I knew she was the girl of my dreams. Or, more accurately, from one of my dreams.

I'd not had any spiritual dreams for a while on my mission until a few months in. Then, one night, I dreamed I'd been taken to heaven, where God had told me I needed a wife to become and do all that I needed to. He showed me a woman standing nearby and said this was her. I couldn't make out her face, which I took to mean I wasn't ready for her to be revealed to me quite yet; I had more work to do. I had tucked that dream away and focused on the mission in the year that followed, but now, at the Bertagnoles' home, I just knew this was her. Seeing Kim, I had this strangest sensation, like I had known her all my life up to that point. And that I wanted to know her for the rest of my life.

Later, as we got to know each other, Kim would share her own story of being prepared for our meeting. She told me that a couple of weeks before she came back to Casper for the weekend with her best friend and college roommate, Sherry, she'd had a dream in which she had seen her father teaching a man who, she somehow just knew, would be her husband, and God told her she would meet him soon.

That first evening in Casper, she wasn't dressed to impress, but she certainly made an impression on me. Trim, blond, sweet. I noticed that her eyeliner matched the mint green of the tee-shirt she wore over gray sweats. I was instantly captivated and half-wondered if, half-hoped that, there was a little sparkle in the brief eye contact we made. It occurred to me that I was fortunate this encounter hadn't happened earlier in my mission: there was no way I would have been able to stay focused. As it was, I had six more weeks to fulfill.

Kim and her pal disappeared downstairs almost immediately. When they returned, Kim had changed into a knee-length jeans skirt that accentuated her trim calves and a nice shirt. She seemed to have applied just a little more makeup and fussed with her hair. *Is that for me?* I wondered.

Over the course of the meal, I learned a little more about her. Kim was the second of the Bertagnole children. While many young women in her church community were content to marry young and start a family, she had ambitions to become an elementary school teacher. Having earned a full-ride music scholarship to the University of Wyoming, she had forgone it to study at Utah State University because her favorite schoolteacher had gone there. It was a decision that would test her determination—by losing some of the financial assistance she would have gotten by staying in Wyoming, she was having to work part-time to pay her way.

Despite my best intentions, I found myself flirting. I thought I was doing so somewhat subtly until my mission partner and I finally said goodnight and headed home—an hour or more past our official curfew, because I hadn't wanted the evening to end.

"Hey, could you guys have flirted any more?" he asked.

"Oh," I said. "Was it that noticeable?"

"Yep."

"Well, I don't know," I said, "but I think I'm going to marry her." I wrote that down in my journal that night.

The next day I went back to the Bertagnoles' place. In the time I'd been in Casper, I had enjoyed the conversations I'd had with Mr. Bertagnole about spiritual things; I appreciated his mix of godliness and down-to-earth wisdom. So, I went over to ask him for a recommendation for a good spiritual book to read. Subtle, right?

To my delight, Kim was home, and her parents were out. I explained why I was there, and she invited me in to wait for her folks to return. We chatted and laughed for a couple of hours, Sherry gamely playing chaperone, and I could tell that there were sparks flying between the two of us.

Back at my lodgings that evening, I called Mrs. Bertagnole to ask when Kim was returning to Utah and whether I might write to her. Although I was finding it hard to keep my mind on mission, I was still trying to follow the rules, which said that you couldn't write to girls in your mission area. Technically, though Kim came from the area I was serving in, she was living in another state, but I wasn't going to try to be cute about it.

In due course, I wrote Kim a four-page letter, telling her more about me and how much I had enjoyed meeting her. I finally knew my feelings were reciprocated when her reply came scented with Magnolia, the same perfume I had complimented her on when we shook hands goodbye, asking what it was. Over the next six weeks, we fell in love by correspondence.

With my mission ending on November 6, Kim came home for a visit over Halloween. It was a cold, cold night when I went over to join the family for dinner, but to me, it seemed like someone had turned the thermostat all the way up high. When I got to hug her briefly when I said good night, I was sure the sparks might start a fire.

What made all this even sweeter was that I hadn't just fallen in love with Kim. I had come to love her parents deeply. They filled something of the family void that I had always carried in me through their warmth and their care. During the last few weeks of my mission, I was over at their home most evenings, enjoying their hospitality and appreciating the time I got to spend with Kim's dad, drawing on his godly wisdom.

The promise of a future with Kim was a desperately needed anchor in the storm when I got back to Louisiana. Feeling adrift with my mission focus behind me and surrounded by the same old chaos at home, it was good to have a sense of something positive to look to out there.

I also got some nudges that made me feel God hadn't abandoned me. I was offered a job back at the grocery store I had worked at previously, where the owner also sold me a nice car that had belonged to a son who had died, for a good deal. Within a short time, I was offered a promotion to a different store, in Shreveport, which meant spending a couple of weeks at another location, in Vicksburg, Mississippi, to learn the ropes. They put me in a nice hotel out on the river, a welcome respite from Mom's couch.

Having spoken with Kim's sister Carrie to find out her likes, I'd put an engagement ring on layaway at a little mom-and-pop jewelers in Ruston. Because I couldn't get any extended time away from work, we arranged for Kim to fly down to visit in January, when I planned to surprise her with a proposal.

> **FEELING ADRIFT WITH MY MISSION FOCUS BEHIND ME AND SURROUNDED BY THE SAME OLD CHAOS AT HOME, IT WAS GOOD TO HAVE A SENSE OF SOMETHING POSITIVE TO LOOK TO OUT THERE.**

Shakespeare said that the path of true love doesn't run smoothly, and he was right. Kim's trip coincided with a crazy ice storm that saw her stuck overnight in Dallas en route. Meanwhile, having been able to arrange for three days off work, I finally got to Shreveport to collect her from the airport after spinning off the road into a ditch on the way.

I spent the night and all the next day at the shuttered airport as the storm continued. At one point, Kim decided to give up and fly home from Dallas before I contacted her mom and begged her to make sure Kim didn't do so. Finally, on the third of my days off, Kim made it to Shreveport. The roads were still bad, and what should have been a ninety-minute ride home turned into an hours-long crawl. There were wrecks everywhere. With daylight fading, we decided it was best not to push things and stopped for the night. We found a cheap hotel where we chastely shared a room, me tossing and turning in the other twin bed.

I'd done what I could to prepare Kim a little for meeting my mom. Some of what I had told her about my childhood had made her eyes go wide because it was so different from her upbringing. I had also told Mom what Kim meant to me and about my hopes and dreams for a future life together. Still, there was no predicting how their first meeting would go.

When we finally got to Quitman, I guided Kim indoors and introduced her to Mom.

"She's not pretty at all," Mom said, looking at her. "You told me she was pretty."

I didn't know whether to snort with laughter or snarl with rage. "Mom!" I objected.

"Well, she's just not pretty," Mom went on. "I'm just being honest."

This wasn't a great way to start a visit, and I could picture things only getting worse. I had to be back at work at 3:30 a.m. the next day, so I slept in Tracy's bed, as she was away, so that the others could sit up later in the family room. Kim ended up sharing a bed with my mom.

Having to work meant I left Kim alone not just with Mom but also with Garry, who, in one of his calmer interludes, was living out on the back porch, which had been boarded in to create a crude small room.

When I headed out for work in the dark, I thought, *God, if Kim is still here when I get back later, I'll know without a shadow of a doubt that she's the one.*

She was, and I did.

A WHOLE LIFE

My proposal plans had been shot to pieces by the storm delays, so that evening, when I got back from work, I took Kim out into the yard, where we had a porch swing. It was good to be alone, just the two of us. After we sat for a while, I stood up, got down on one knee, and asked her to marry me. I said the ring was on layaway, but I'd get it as soon as possible.

Kim smiled at me. "I'll think about it," she said. Then she leaned over and, at her instigation, we kissed for the first time. That night, I lay on the couch, unable to sleep, utterly confused. Had the reality of my crazy family given Kim second thoughts?

When I finished work the following day, Kim and I finally got to go out on our first-ever date. We ate at El Chico's, my favorite Mexican restaurant in Ruston. Then we went to see a movie. There wasn't much of a selection, so we ended up buying tickets for *Fatal Attraction*;[30] for me, a crazy drama that was not that far-fetched. Not exactly the most romantic choice, however. On the drive home, I finally got up the courage to ask Kim if she had thought about my proposal.

"Oh yes," she said with a smile. "I'll marry you! I knew pretty much from the day that we met I was going to marry you."

I was delighted, thrilled, and confused. "So why did you make me wait like this?"

"Because I knew no girl had ever said no to you before," she said, her smile widening to a grin. "I needed to put you in your place first!"

No other girl had ever spoken like that to me before, and I realized that I liked it. Here was someone who was not only cute

---

30 Adrian Lyne, *Fatal Attraction* (September 18, 1987; Jaffe-Lansing Productions).

and caring but courageous and clear-minded—someone I could build a lifetime with.

I gave Kim her engagement ring at a big Valentine's Day dance in Casper. Not long after her visit to Louisiana, I had quit my job, packed up my car with all my belongings, and headed north to Wyoming.

Kim still had eighteen months of schooling to finish, but we decided it made the most sense for her to transfer back to Casper to complete it there, where there were more job prospects for me than out in Utah. Kim's parents had said I could live in the small guest house on their property. Within a day of arriving, I'd secured a position at a local grocery store.

I'd known the Bertagnoles had warmed to me, but I wasn't certain that they would approve of our getting married. After all, they had heard me tell something of my wayward path, a far different life to the one their daughter had known. Any doubts were dismissed when I called Kim's father to ask permission to propose.

"Do you feel like you've been forgiven for all your past sins?" he asked. "And do you think you're good enough for my daughter?"

"I know I've been forgiven," I said. "And I think I am good enough for Kim. I still have some growing to do, but I'll get where I need to be with her help."

"Well," Mr. Bertagnole said, "if you feel like God has forgiven you, who am I to judge you? Yes, you can marry my daughter."

I wouldn't have blamed him for having reservations. After all, my chaotic background hadn't laid the foundations for healthy relationships. But over the past two years, while on my mission, I had been exposed to many positive examples, spending time with different couples and families who modeled love and faithfulness.

Still, I had a few rough edges, one of which needed ironing out before Kim and I exchanged our vows. We were heading to get our formal engagement photographs taken when she told me she was going out with Sherry the following night, a Friday. This was our usual date night, so I complained, and we got into our first big fight.

Somehow, the photographer managed to coax some persuasive smiles out of us during our session, but things were still tense when we left. On the way home, I said petulantly, "You know, Kim, maybe we should call off the wedding."

"What?" she said. "Why?"

"Well, I don't think you're going to be subservient enough." It's embarrassing to admit now, but that's actually what I told her.

"Well, then maybe you're right," Kim shot back. "If that's what you're looking for, you have come to the wrong place."

As we parted, Kim walking to the main house and me heading to the guest house, it looked like our wedding date four weeks away was off.

Later that evening, Kim's father came over to see me. He spoke kindly but firmly at the same time. He told me how muddle-headed I was, that a husband and wife were equal partners, and Kim wasn't going to be second fiddle to anyone.

"Is that what you really want?" he asked.

"No, sir," I told him. "I was just stupid; I got mad."

"Well, you'd better get over there and apologize and tell her you'll never say anything like that again," he told me. "Don't make me regret giving you her hand."

It took me just a few minutes to do the first part of what he said; I told her how sorry I was, and Kim was gracious and forgiving. Though he has since passed, sadly, I'm still working hard every day to fulfill Kim's father's second direction to me.

CHAPTER 18

We settled into married life happily in Casper. No one from my family had been at the wedding: Mom had said she would come but called a couple of days before the ceremony to tell me she didn't think their car would make the long trip and they couldn't afford the gas. I'd sent an invitation to Uncle Sonny, care of Huntsville Prison, Texas, but he was understandably a no-show. A couple of years later, Kim got to meet him for the first time at Garry's funeral. He hugged her. "Thanks for the wedding invite, by the way. Sorry, I couldn't make it," he said with a grin. "I tried like hell, but they caught me."

Part of me was disappointed that I had no family there when I exchanged vows with Kim, but another part of me accepted it as par for the course. And I realized that my family's absence was in some ways symbolic: I was leaving all that craziness behind to start a new family of my own, one for which I wanted stability and security. I was beginning a whole new life.

I'd gotten a job in the produce department at an Albertsons, while Kim was working at a daycare with plans to finish her teaching degree. We'd rented a small apartment, and while we didn't have much money, we were content and excited for the future. And then things changed with the unplanned arrival of our first baby before even our first anniversary.

With Kim no longer working, our finances were even tighter. We ate a lot of ramen noodles, and we were always welcome at Kim's parents' house for a meal, so we survived. We were getting by, but we knew it wasn't a long-term solution; something needed to change in our circumstances. The break came with the offer of a produce manager's position at another Albertsons. The only drawback was that it was in Denver, a long way from Casper and Kim's family. Also, I knew that even with a raise, we wouldn't be able to afford the rent out there. Kim's friend Sherry came up with a solution. She told us she'd been offered a job out in Denver, too, and had been wondering what to do: how about we shared an apartment out there?

We were in Denver for just over a year. Living with Sherry worked out fine, but Kim never settled in the bigger city, where she felt unsafe. And when we discovered that she was expecting again, we knew we needed to be back nearer to her family. Unfortunately, there were no openings at Albertsons back there, but I found a job as a rep with Frito-Lay.

I started out as a vacation filler for the state, which meant I stepped in for any of the other regular guys when they were taking time off. I'd be sent out for a week to somewhere like Cody, where I'd be put up for a week in a hotel while I subbed. It could be lonely, so sometimes Kim would bring the kids and come with me.

The discipline I'd learned during my church mission prepared me for what was a demanding job. They were typically twelve-hour days, starting at three o'clock in the morning. Even a van full of chips doesn't weigh much, so in the winter you had to be careful out on icy roads because the vehicle didn't have much traction. More than once, I'd thought that my time was up as I wrestled to keep the truck on the road.

In addition to the long hours, I also had to draw on and develop my salesman skills. I was always looking to secure a good end cap on which to stack my chips—prime grocery store real estate. That meant persuading the department manager that my chips would sell better than other brands and making sure my shelf space was always stocked. At some of the busier stores, that meant going back two or even three times a day to check on things, tidy up, and restock as needed.

After about a year or so of bouncing around like this, a permanent route became open. It was in Rawlins, a small town best known for being the location of the Wyoming State Penitentiary. The prison was one of my stops. Once I was admitted, I wasn't allowed to touch anything: I'd open up the back of the truck, and the inmates would unload the delivery. The chips were tastier than much of the regular prison food that got served up, so there'd always be some laughing and joking.

One of the guards I got to know observed one time that I seemed more at ease in the prison than many of the other outsiders who had to visit for one reason or another. "Well, I spent quite a bit of time visiting relatives inside when I was growing up," I told him. That led to an invitation for me to go in one day and speak to some of the inmates for a few minutes. I talked about how I'd been going down the wrong road when I was younger, until I found God, and how I hoped they would discover Him, too.

Delivering there was a reminder of how different my life had turned out from the way it could have been, especially one drop in January 1992: I drove out there on the day of the last execution at the prison. None of the inmates looked at me and talked, as they usually did, and there was a heaviness over the whole place.

When we discovered our third child was on the way, a route came open in Casper, and we were glad to be back near Kim's family. Her parents let us live in their guest house for a time so we could save up enough money to put toward a house.

And so the years went by. It seemed like no time had passed before we had five children, and I'd been with Frito-Lay for eight years. Though we were healthy and happy, life was full. I was still grinding twelve-hour days, and I'd need to be in bed by seven o'clock to be up bright and early the following day.

Driving between deliveries gave me plenty of time to think, and as I looked ahead, I realized that something needed to change. I was making enough money to get by, but we weren't getting ahead. My children never went to bed hungry like I had, but we didn't eat fancy a lot. We took day trips and had fun, but things like going to Disney were a pipe dream. And what about as they grew—paying for missions service assignments of their own, maybe, or college? There weren't a lot of prospects for advancement with Frito-Lay.

"We need to find something where you can use your gift of the gab," Kim said one day as we sat mulling over my options. What that looked like came in the Sunday paper (which I didn't steal but had delivered). Kim spotted an advert recruiting agents for Farmers Insurance.

Our insurance was with Prudential, where I knew the agent because he had previously been at Frito-Lay with me. "All he does is talk a lot, and we hand him a check," said Kim. "How hard can that be?"

My resume wasn't particularly impressive. In addition to sales rep, I listed dishwasher, garbageman, and waterbed salesman—a gig I'd had for a few months on returning to Casper from Denver before the Frito-Lay spot opened up. We hemmed and hawed about whether to mention my church mission under "extra activities."

"Why not?" said Kim. "You went door to door and sold religion for two years. They might think that if you can do that, then you can surely sell insurance."

A week or so later, I got a call from Ken, the Farmers district manager. "I got your resume, young man," he told me. "And honestly, it's probably the most pathetic resume I have ever seen." My heart dropped as I realized this was just a courtesy call to count me out.

"The only reason I'm calling you is this church mission thing," he went on. "Tell me more about that."

I told him about going door to door, asking people if they wanted to talk about religion. About getting turned down, taking a deep breath, and then going to the next door and asking again. He invited me in for an interview, where I got to tell him about being shot at, having boiling water thrown at me, and a big dog sicced on me. He thought that was pretty funny.

"You know what," he said, "I'm going to give you a shot. Most new insurance agents fail because they can't handle rejection, but it sounds like you've had a bit of practice!"

Kim didn't only open this new door for me; she helped me step through it. Before I could start training with Farmers and earn commission, I had to get my property and casualty license—at my own expense. I'd finish my day job with Frito-Lay, go home and spend some time with the family, then study late before grabbing a few hours' sleep and starting all over again.

After two weeks of cramming, I went to the test center and bombed. You needed a seventy to pass, and I made sixty-four. Dejected, I went home and told Kim maybe this wasn't such a good idea. Perhaps I should stick to delivering chips.

Kim wasn't having any of it. She reminded me we had both prayed about this opportunity and felt like it was something we should pursue. That didn't mean it would be easy, though, she went on; I needed to stick with it.

While I had never been a great test-taker at school, Kim was a straight-A student. She tutored me over the next couple of weeks, and when I went back to retake it, I passed. Delighted, I called Ken to tell him I was ready to start, only to learn of another hurdle. Things had changed, he told me, and I now needed to pass my life and health license, too, before I could start earning.

Knuckling down, I hit the books again for two weeks and returned to the test center. Sixty-nine. So close, and I was frustrated: these tests were costing us precious time and money. I immediately rebooked another test for the next day. I stayed up all night studying, went to work, then headed for the test center. Sixty-nine again! This time, I was done. I told Kim maybe we'd misread the signs. Perhaps these results were God's way of telling us insurance wasn't for me.

"No," she said. "You're so close. We can get you there." I scheduled another test for two weeks out. Kim coached and encouraged me in the days leading up, and I walked out having scored a seventy-one. We were on track!

If I had any lingering doubts about the path we were pursuing, they were reinforced when I went to tell my Frito-Lay manager I was leaving. "Selling insurance?" he said. "Do you know how hard that is?" He went on to tell me about all the people he knew who had tried to make a go of it in that field and failed. "And you're going to give up the security of a regular paycheck for who knows what?"

When I discovered that the base salary I would be making at Farmers was less than I had initially been led to believe, I began to have serious second thoughts. I told Kim maybe I should stay at Frito-Lay and just sell insurance in the evenings.

"There's no way you can do both, and I'm not going to watch you kill yourself," Kim said. "And besides, if you give part-time effort, you're going to get part-time results."

I knew she was right, but I felt overwhelmed by the responsibility of providing. How were we going to pay the mortgage and feed the children, I asked?

"I tell you what, Jack," Kim said. "Let me worry about that. You're not going to look at another bill that comes into this house, okay? You let me handle the mortgage and the food. We've got credit cards we can use until you're up and running."

That was the inspiration and the motivation that I needed: Kim believed in me, and I didn't want to let her down. If leaving Frito-Lay was a leap of faith, it was one we were taking together, hand in hand.

True to her word, Kim took over our domestic finances and made every effort not to let on how stressful it was for her, freeing me to focus on making a go of things as an insurance agent.

> **THAT WAS THE INSPIRATION AND THE MOTIVATION THAT I NEEDED: KIM BELIEVED IN ME, AND I DIDN'T WANT TO LET HER DOWN.**

There was just one flicker on her determined face. At the end of my first month with Farmers, I received my base check—for $302. I took it home and presented it to Kim.

"Well, that's not bad for your first week," she said encouragingly.

I paused. "Actually, honey, that's for the month, remember?"

She didn't say anything negative, but I caught what I felt was a momentary look of fear on her face. I determined that I would do whatever it took to ensure that never happened again.

CHAPTER 19

Having squeaked through my insurance exams, I knew that I wasn't going to excel in my new career on smarts alone. But I was determined that no one was going to outwork me. What I lacked in giftedness, I was going to make up for in sheer doggedness. I may not have a lot of great in me, but I had plenty of grit.

I started by sticking to my Frito-Lay hours. The Farmers office didn't open until 9 a.m. but I was up and at the grocery stores I used to deliver chips to by 4 a.m. to tap into my first potential circle of business: people I already knew. I'd stand out at the back as they wheeled their inventory in, chat for a few moments if they had time, and ask them about their insurance needs. From there, I'd head to the office at about 6:30 a.m. to note any follow-up actions I needed to take care of and prepare my to-do list for the day, then start my cold calls from 8 a.m.

I'd take an apple and a granola bar for lunch, so I didn't have to leave my desk to go and get something to eat—midday was prime calling time because people were more likely to answer their phones when they were on their break. Or they might even be willing to meet in person if I could run out to where they were located. I would keep working the phones through the end of the day and then get home in time to have dinner with Kim and the kids and have some daddy time. After we had eaten and played a bit, I'd go down into the basement and spend an hour or two making more calls, often with a little one sitting on my lap.

> **WHAT I LACKED IN GIFTEDNESS, I WAS GOING TO MAKE UP FOR IN SHEER DOGGEDNESS. I MAY NOT HAVE A LOT OF GREAT IN ME, BUT I HAD PLENTY OF GRIT.**

I've learned that many agents hate cold calling, but I loved it from the start. It brought back some of the sense of challenge and opportunity I'd experienced during my mission, never knowing what you would find on the other side of that door you had just knocked on. Besides, I'd paid for many of these leads—their contact details came from some internet inquiry form they had filled in—and I wasn't going to throw that money away too quickly.

Just as I'd done when I was out knocking on doors, I'd look for a way to make a connection before getting down to business. Obviously, there weren't the kind of visual clues I would get walking up someone's driveway, but I would look for other openings. "Are you from Wyoming?" was one. No, they might say, they were from Connecticut or New York or wherever. "Oh," I'd respond. "I've never been there. I hear that it's great there."

Or, if it were somewhere I knew of, I'd throw in a little tidbit that showed I knew what I was talking about. Then I'd ask what brought them to Wyoming and about their families.

I'd also have my ears open for clues—for instance, when I asked for someone's social security number. If it didn't start with 520, I knew they were out of state: in the least-populated state in the country, everyone in Wyoming had the same first three digits.

Hopefully, in one way or another, we'd made some sort of a connection within a few minutes, and I could pivot. "I can't remember why I called. . . . oh yeah, you were looking for insurance, right?"

I quickly realized that Mondays and Fridays were not good days for cold-calling, Mondays because people were bummed about having to go back to work and focused on all that they had to get done, Fridays because they were tired at the end of a busy week, and looking forward to the weekend.

Some agents I knew were kind of relieved if they made a cold call and no one answered; they would write it off as a no-go. My attitude was I was going to keep calling until I got to speak with someone. I would leave a voicemail and call back, leave another voicemail and call back. I figured, *I have paid for this lead, and I am going to try to work it until you tell me to get lost.*

A guy did that once, only in slightly more colorful and emphatic language. I took his tone as an indicator that I should scratch him off my list! But the next day, I thought, *What the heck? I'm going to call him back one more time. What's the worst that can happen; he can double-cuss me out?*

I spoke quickly when he answered my call, so he didn't have time to interject. "Hi there, Jack Jameson. Look, I know you told me to eff off last night, which is fine, but I just wondered: did you really mean that, or were you just having a bad day?" The man chuckled. "You know, I'd had a bad day at work, and my wife was on me about something when you called," he told me. He said he respected me for calling again, and we went on to write him a policy.

That encounter underscored for me that a "no" may just be for now, not forever. But if you aren't persistent, if you don't persevere, if you won't keep at it, you will miss out on all those potential opportunities. I reminded myself that every no I got took me one call closer to my next yes.

Pretty quickly, I was achieving a fifty percent closing rate on internet leads—about double the usual—but there were enough setbacks to keep me from getting too confident. One particular situation highlighted for me how determination is great, but you have to have the basics down. You must be able to follow through on what you promise.

> **IF YOU AREN'T PERSISTENT, IF YOU DON'T PERSEVERE, IF YOU WON'T KEEP AT IT, YOU WILL MISS OUT ON ALL THOSE POTENTIAL OPPORTUNITIES.**

I was writing my largest policy to date with a guy I had met at one of my early morning grocery stops. We were bundling his home and auto policies, which included coverage for his teenage boys. When he came into the office with his check, I submitted an online proposal to confirm the details we had discussed. I felt the blood drain out of my face when it came back fifty percent higher than I had quoted him. Trying not to look panicked, I told him I needed to call head office to confirm something. When I got through to someone there, trying to look calm as the man sat across the desk from me, I was told I'd made a mistake. I had put in the wrong code for his kids, identifying them as girls, for whom coverage was lower because young male drivers were a greater risk.

With a knot in my stomach, I hung up and told the man what I'd done wrong. "I'm very sorry," I said, confirming the higher premium. "I'm pretty new at all this...."

The guy reached for the check he had laid on my desk, picked it up, and ripped it into little pieces. Then he threw them up in the air like confetti. "Quit wasting my time," he said as he got up and walked out. "Call me when you know what you're doing."

I felt sick, but I never made that mistake again. And a year later, the man called me back. The company he had gone with instead of Farmers had made a significant rate increase, and he wanted to know what we could do for him. I double-checked my work and quoted him a premium he signed for.

Starting out, I knew that I needed every contract I could sign, no matter how small, to build up some kind of a head of steam. So, on Saturdays, I would go out to sell renter's insurance. Now, this didn't make much money—maybe only $10 or

$12 a time—but I reckoned that enough of those would add up to something. Plus, it was keeping me busy and keeping me positive. Better to be out there knocking on doors expectantly than sitting at my desk drumming my fingers anxiously. It gave me some sense of control over my future: I wasn't just going to sit and hope for the best; I was going to go out and try to make something happen.

I went to apartment complexes and methodically knocked on each door from 9 a.m. to 5 p.m. It turned out to be fertile ground because I discovered that around ninety percent of tenants had no insurance. They just assumed that their landlord covered them. A big mistake!

Then I came across a news article in the Sunday paper about a guy renting a unit in a fourplex. He left a pot of shrimp on the stove when he went out, and the resulting fire burned not only his apartment but the one next door. He had no insurance, nor did his neighbors, who then sued him for their losses. It was quite an object lesson. I cut the article out, glued it to a piece of construction paper, and carried it with me as a piece of show and tell when someone answered the door. That poor guy's experience won me a lot of business.

However, even with my Saturday efforts and working my personal connections and internet leads hard during the week, I knew I needed to expand my circles of potential business. Sometimes, there are opportunities right in front of our noses if we only take a moment to look. I started taking different routes to the office, looking out for different businesses I passed and could visit. I dictated notes to myself on my cell phone to remember the details.

I WASN'T JUST GOING TO SIT AND HOPE FOR THE BEST; I WAS GOING TO GO OUT AND TRY TO MAKE SOMETHING HAPPEN.

I realized that people like to do business with people who do business with them. So, if I ate at a restaurant, I'd ask the wait staff if the owner was in. If they were, I would say hello and introduce myself. I wouldn't take much of their time; I'd just tell them I was in insurance and that if they were unhappy with their present situation, I'd be glad to speak with them. If they showed any interest, I would also offer to have a look at their existing policy and give them a free review. I would ask them their renewal date and make a note in my calendar. Then, a month or so ahead, I would drop by and remind them their renewal was coming up, and I could review things for them if they wanted. If someone told me their policy was at home, I might offer to swing by when I was in the area and have a look.

There were a couple of reasons for my persistence here. First, business insurance earns more significant commissions than domestic. But it also opens up other doors. When you write someone's business insurance, you can then serve their domestic needs, which can add up when you consider life, house, and auto insurance. And then there is the best return of all—the likelihood of a personal endorsement to someone else. When someone recommends "my guy"—whether that's a doctor, a landscaper, an attorney, or an insurance agent—to you, that's a high-value connection. And referrals aren't only more meaningful, they are also free!

I thought about the different ways people connected with others. For example, most homeowners have mortgages, so I started visiting mortgage brokerages. I'd drop off a box of donuts or some other kind of treat and leave some of my business cards for people to pass on. When I had a moment to chat, I'd observe that I knew when people were on a tight budget, homeowner's insurance that was too pricey could break a mortgage deal. "If you've got someone who's on the verge of not qualifying for a loan because their homeowner's insurance needs to be lower, I'm not promising I can help, but I will do everything I can to make it work," I would tell them.

I also took donuts to local realtors. I asked if I might get to speak for a few minutes at one of their agents' meetings, and when I got the opportunity, I would address one of their felt needs—such as helping prospective clients who might be having trouble getting insurance because of previous claims they had made.

One day, I was driving past a fire station on my way to the office when I decided to stop and visit. Chatting with one of the guys about what I did, he told me the city provided firefighters with life insurance coverage, but it was for only $30,000. That wasn't going to go very far. I asked if I could bring pizza and soda one day and talk to the crews about how they might want to consider taking better care of their families in the event of a tragedy. When that presentation went well, I visited all the other fire stations in town—and then did the same thing with the police.

All of these different efforts began to pay off. After a shaky first month, when I brought home that check for just $302 that made Kim nervous, I soon hit my stride. At the end of my first full year, I had earned twice what I had been making after eight years with Frito-Lay. When I sat down to review my progress with the office manager, she told me that I had already made the numbers that were required of me by the end of my second year—an unprecedented achievement. Not bad for someone with just a high school diploma. In my fourth year, I earned more in a month than in an entire year delivering chips.

CHAPTER 20

It's been said that behind every successful man is a surprised woman, but if I can claim to have accomplished anything, that snarky comment is not true in my case. Kim has always believed in me more than I believe in myself, and she is so much of the reason for the fulfilling life we have enjoyed together.

I can't emphasize enough how vital her support has been. Indeed, when I speak to other agents about building their business, I make a point of stressing the importance of having a significant other of some kind. It could be a spouse, a relative, or a close friend, but you must have some sort of a support system, someone who is there for you when it gets hard.

I may have been the front-of-house guy in the spotlight, but she was the behind-the-scenes person ensuring everything ran smoothly. Even with all my marketing efforts, there would be days when I would come home without having secured a policy, and I would be discouraged. Like a second in a boxer's corner, she would patch me up, whisper some encouragement, give me a neck rub, slap me on the back, and then send me out for the next round.

Though our income went up pretty quickly, clearing some of our debts meant that it took some time until we began to enjoy the benefits, so Kim kept a close eye on the finances. She would take her calculator down to the grocery store to make sure we were staying within budget and became very creative with ramen menus. Later, she would tell me more about that day I had come home with the check for just $302. After she had told me she would handle the money side of things from then on, she'd gone into the bedroom, knelt, and prayed for God's help because she didn't know how she was going to manage. But she never let on to me about her fears because she didn't want to burden me.

With business taking off, I needed help with some of the back-end office stuff, but we weren't yet doing well enough to employ someone. I needed a person who was licensed, so Kim studied and went and passed her tests the first time (bettering my efforts) so she could be my unpaid secretary.

Having Kim's help on the administrative side of things gave me more time to expand my marketing efforts further. I got an idea from something I had started doing with the firefighters and the police. Hearing their stories about dealing with distraught children when they responded to emergency calls, I remembered how comforting Honey Bunny had been to me when I was small and fearful. So, I ordered a bunch of small teddies in little firefighter or police uniforms—with my name and contact details on a small tab—for the first responders to distribute to kids in need.

Then, I visited the children's departments at the local hospitals with the same offer. They loved the idea, and I made sure to drop off only a few bears when I visited, so I'd have to go back regularly to top up their supply—providing me another opportunity to build relationships with people. In time, I started getting inquiries from doctors, nurses, and other staff wanting help with their personal insurance needs.

That was neat, of course, but most rewarding was the call I got one day from a number I did not recognize. A woman wanted to know if I was "the teddy bear guy" because she had a story to tell. She and her husband had moved to Wyoming from California just a few months previously, she explained. Soon after, she and her husband and their two small children were involved in a serious car accident. The little ones were okay, but Mom and Dad were pretty badly hurt and needed surgery. While they were in the ER, nursing staff gave each kid one of my bears to help them feel safe.

"Neither of my children will go to bed without their bear," she told me. Learning where they had come from, she wanted to say thank you, she went on. "And I told my husband, 'Anyone who would do something that kind, I want them to be our insurance agent.' Can you take over all our policies?"

I told the woman I was pleased to hear that those bears had been a help to her family and that I'd be happy to get some information, research some quotes, and get back to her.

"Oh no," she said. "You don't understand. I don't care what the price is. I just want you to be our insurance agent."

That conversation captures the essence of my whole approach over the past twenty or so years—that insurance, ultimately, is not just about numbers. It's about connection and relationship. People are putting their lives and the lives of their families in my hands, in a sense, and they need to be confident they can trust me.

That perspective guided a couple of decisions I made early on. One was that I would never write an auto insurance policy for the state minimum. I explained to prospective clients that the low premiums they may have been quoted elsewhere were based on the minimum insurance required by law in the state. And while that might meet a legal standard, it probably wouldn't help them if they did get involved in an auto claim.

It was simple math: at that time, Wyoming required drivers to have coverage of at least $25,000 per person, $50,000 for an accident, and $10,000 for medical. "You do realize there are trucks out there that cost more than all of that combined?" I would point out. "If you hit one of them, insurance only has to pay what your limits are. Anything else is going to come out of your pocket." I explained how they could be sued for any balance, maybe even lose their home, or have their wages garnered.

"You don't have to be a millionaire to be sued like one," I'd say. "If you are underinsured and you do get sued, I'm going to feel terrible, and I can't live with that. So, I'm not going to under-insure you to get your money. An extra $20 a month now is going to be better than having to find $100,000 someday."

I lost some business as a result, but far more frequently, I had people thank me for explaining what was really going on. They were happy to take my advice and increase their coverage.

Before too long, I didn't need to pay for internet leads anymore: I had plenty of referrals. But I knew I needed to keep my name out there, so I looked for sponsorship opportunities and found no shortage. As my kids got older and joined different sports leagues, I'd help support them. When Kim started a cardio kickboxing class at the gym, I offered to provide Farmers tee-shirts and gym bags for all the women taking part.

I also looked for opportunities to have a presence at community events. I sponsored the motorcycle riding courses run at the local Harley Davidson dealers, setting up a stand with giveaway bandannas. That gave me a chance to explain to new riders that basic insurance wouldn't cover a well-tricked-out bike if there was any serious damage. Realizing that Saturdays were a big day for RV dealers, I'd take in breakfast for the sales reps and set up a booth to speak with prospective buyers about their insurance needs.

One of my most out-of-the-box ideas was renting a booth at Casper's annual health fair. I paid a premium rate for a spot right by the stall where people picked up the results of free blood testing that was being offered. When they walked by with their paperwork, I'd smile and call out, "How were your results? Good or bad?"

It was a little cheeky, for sure, and one or two people looked at me a bit oddly, but most were okay with my friendly tone. If they said their results were great, I would tell them that was good news because they qualified for our best rate in life insurance. If they said their results were not so good, I'd tell them I had a particular life insurance policy that could not decline anyone and ask if were they interested. Even Kim, my greatest supporter, thought the health fair booth was a step too far when I first pitched it to her, but I ended up writing six policies from the event. Not a bad day's work at all.

Many of these public events were family affairs for us, for a couple of reasons. For one thing, I at least got to spend some time with Kim and the children. I could take a break and visit with them for a while, and they enjoyed exploring whatever might be happening. And I found that children were a great draw to a booth. Who will refuse a pamphlet offered by a cute six-year-old girl?

The children thing worked both ways, I discovered. Offering free helium balloons was an instant draw, and I quickly learned to make sure that when Kim was helping me by inflating them, she didn't do it too quickly: if she took her time, that gave me an opportunity to chat with the kid's parents for a while.

I also recognized that there is an art to working at a public event. How many times have you walked by a booth where someone is sitting down behind their table looking bored or, worse, scrolling on their cell phone? You might skim their table to see if there are any good freebies, but you're not likely to want to get into much of a conversation. If they aren't interested in what they are selling, why should you be? So, I would always be on my feet, saying hi or holding out some of our giveaways.

Good marketing isn't just about finding new clients. It also means holding on to the ones that you have. And not just for their repeat business but for the word-of-mouth business they produce through recommending you to their friends. That means more than just an annual call when it's time for them to renew their policy.

I started by sending out birthday cards, wishing clients well, and thanking them for their business. One time, I was in Walmart when a guy came up to me whom I recognized as a client.

"Hey, Jack," he said. "Thank you for the birthday card. I got divorced a couple of years ago, and I just turned fifty. I was feeling kinda depressed. . . . no one else acknowledged my birthday, but I got your card, and that meant a lot to me."

Then, I extended the birthday card thing to clients' children. After all, I figured, they were part of the reason for my client relationship in the first place, and they were also my potential future clients. I would throw in a sheet of stickers with the card as a small gift. It was amazing how many clients would tell me how much their kids loved getting those cards in the mail.

> **GOOD MARKETING ISN'T JUST ABOUT FINDING NEW CLIENTS. IT ALSO MEANS HOLDING ON TO THE ONES THAT YOU HAVE.**

All this took some organizing. As business grew and I took on staff, we used a customer management system that helped us keep track of all the details. Any time someone from the team had a conversation with someone, they would write a few notes anyone could refer to. If someone came into the office, I'd scan those details to freshen my memory so I could make some personal reference.

Remembering how much those Salvation Army Christmas gifts meant to me as a kid, I decided I wanted to do something to help families who were struggling at the holidays. Together with my staff, we identified three families from our client list we knew were having a hard time—maybe the dad had just got laid off, or there was some kind of serious sickness—and would be sure they celebrated a great Christmas, with good food and gifts.

That was meaningful for the families we chose, naturally, but it was only for a handful of people and only once a year. I initiated other practices to expand the number of clients we interacted with. I gave my team members each a $10 or $20 gas card every week and challenged them to find a deserving recipient. We also instituted a call hour, during which they got to phone as many clients as possible to say hello and thanks for their business. Sometimes, they might get tied up with an elderly, lonely client who was glad to have someone to speak to for a while; if so, that was fine, too. It was all about making sure as much as possible that our customers had more warm touches than cold touches from us over the year.

If the only time they heard from us was when their coverage came up for renewal, and we were informing them about a rate increase, it would be understandable if they decided to shop around for someone else to help them. But if they felt that we genuinely cared about them, they would likely stay with us.

Naturally, that meant everything we did had to be sincere, not just sales talk. We had to be willing to deliver on our commitment to help. For example, more than once, when I called a client just to say hi, I learned that they were moving house that coming weekend. So, I hired a truck and turned up to help them.

One of the things I did that was different when I was starting out was put my cell phone number on my business cards. I didn't want clients calling an 800 number after hours or on the weekend when they needed help and getting no answer. When you need to call your insurance company, it's usually because you are in a stressful situation, and you don't need any barriers to getting the help you need.

"I don't want you calling me at eight o'clock at night on a Tuesday asking me how much your renewal premium is going to be," I'd said with a laugh, "but I'm going to be upset if you have a bad house fire or get in a bad car accident, and somebody's hurt, somebody's in the hospital, and you don't call me!"

My phone rang at two o'clock one morning and there was a client on the other end, sobbing. She had been out for the evening with a friend and when she got back to where she had parked her car, she discovered it had been totaled. To be honest, I was kind of glad to hear that because she sounded a bit tipsy, and I wouldn't have wanted her to be driving around. I just told her I was glad she was okay, that was the main thing, and she should get some sleep and call me in the morning when we could get everything worked out.

If someone called me after a traffic accident during office hours and I wasn't tied up with an appointment, I'd ask where they were. If they were close enough, I'd jump in my car and drive out to the scene to help them fill out the police report and make sure everything was in order for a subsequent claim. One hot July afternoon, I went out to help a young mom who had been in an accident with her two-year-old son in the back of the vehicle. Naturally, she was a bit shaken up, so I was pleased to be able to have them sit in my air-conditioned car while the police did their thing, and then I drove them home.

Why go the extra mile like that, literally? Because I wanted to do everything I could to separate myself from the competition. If someone's premium was going to increase on renewal because they had made a claim, I wanted to give them every reason to stick with me because they knew I would take care of them. If it's just about being the cheapest option, chances are there will always be someone who is willing to undersell you.

CHAPTER 21

Like when I'd been out on my church mission, I hadn't been selling insurance too long before I found my name starting to get around as my results drew leaders' attention. People higher up the totem pole in Farmers started asking, "Who is this Jack Jameson?" How was I beating out other, more experienced agents, especially in a small town in a small state where there were twice as many antelopes as people?

I made Farmers Toppers Club for the top ten percent of agents in the country my first year and every year after that. My first award was for writing our region's most auto insurance policies: a trip to a NASCAR race anywhere we wanted. Kim and I chose California because we had never been there. It was the first of many reward trips we would get to take for high performance in the coming years—Europe, Hawaii, and across the contiguous United States. I made the elite President's Council—honoring the top hundred or so agents nationwide, from all 12,000 in the company—for eight consecutive years. I also earned a place at the million-dollar round table, an industry-wide honor for top life insurance sales. At those five-star gatherings, there was a red-carpet reception, fine dining, and top-class entertainment. I'll never forget the first time I got to take the whole family to Disneyland. Walking through the entrance gates with all five of my children wide-eyed and filled with wonder made me feel so good. I wanted them to enjoy all the things I hadn't got to experience when I was their age.

It was all a far cry from the days of secondhand clothes, one slice of bologna in the fridge, and a single weekend with my dad. I was so proud and grateful to be able to celebrate having come so far with Kim and our children.

I'd only been in business eighteen months or so when I first got asked to share some of my secret sauce with other agents from across Wyoming and Montana who came to Casper for a day. Then, I got an invitation to go to Columbus, Ohio, where I spoke to a crowd of around four hundred. Almost before I knew it, I was being asked to travel all over the place. This turned out to be even more rewarding than the leadership honors. I found that I enjoyed sharing some of what I had learned and helping others succeed.

The big challenge with all the speaking engagements I was offered was balancing all the invitations I was receiving with keeping my own business going. Although I'd been able to take on staff, I couldn't be gone too long. I realized that if I wanted to grow my business, I needed to let go of some things. Sure, the person I hired may not be able to do what I did, certainly to begin with. But suppose they could achieve even 70-80 percent of what I did, with the potential to improve.

In that case, they were freeing me up to focus on new opportunities or more critical responsibilities, which was worth it. In my case, that meant letting someone else handle home and auto insurance while I focused more on my great passion, life insurance.

I always say that life policies are the real test of a great insurance agent. Why? Because, by law, if you are buying a home, you have to have home insurance, and if you drive a car, you have to have auto insurance. So, in some ways, you may say that you're not really selling it to someone, you're just the person they choose to buy from. But no law says you need to have life insurance; that's a choice. And it is one I am passionate about.

At the end of the day, insurance is about protecting your assets. Most of us think of that in terms of possessions—the house, the car, and so on. But actually, you are your most important asset.

Think about it. If you're married, chances are the mortgage you have on your house is calculated on two incomes, if you are both working, as many couples are these days. So, what is going to happen if, heaven forbid, you die unexpectedly? Your spouse isn't going to be able to keep up with the payments on their own. Now, in addition to their grief over losing you, they are having to face losing their home. Multiply the stress of that by several factors if you have children.

The reason most agents don't like to broach the subject of life insurance is that it brings up an uncomfortable topic: mortality. But I believe it is better to experience a little discomfort now to avoid a whole lot more in the future. In fact, when I speak on the subject to agents, I maintain that I believe they have a moral obligation to raise the issue with their clients.

The fact of the matter is that around 40 percent of Americans don't have any life insurance and somewhere around 70 percent do not have enough money on hand to even be able to pay for a loved one's funeral. That means putting it on a credit card.

Now, not only do you have to pay interest until that charge is paid off, but each time your monthly statement comes in, you are reminded of one of the most painful experiences of your life.

> **AT THE END OF THE DAY, INSURANCE IS ABOUT PROTECTING YOUR ASSETS. MOST OF US THINK OF THAT IN TERMS OF POSSESSIONS—THE HOUSE, THE CAR, AND SO ON. BUT ACTUALLY, YOU ARE YOUR MOST IMPORTANT ASSET.**

Some people say that when it comes to bereavement, money isn't important because it can never bring that person back. It's true that they can never be replaced, but having adequate insurance sure makes living with grief easier in some ways for those who are left behind. I'm haunted by that reality with one of my clients.

I was in the office one day when a young woman came in. She was heavily pregnant, with a little boy in tow, and she looked drawn and crushed. I didn't recognize her, but when she told me her last name, I realized I had dealt with her husband, who was a welder in the oil industry.

She told me that he had recently been killed in a tragic work accident. His life insurance through work was only around $10,000, just enough to cover the funeral, and she wanted to know about the other arrangements he had made with me.

My heart sank. I remembered the times I had spoken to him about the need for life insurance, but he had shrugged it off. All I had written was car and home insurance coverage.

"I'm so sorry," I told the young widow with a tight throat. "He had nothing with us...."

The heartache didn't end there. A few months later, she called to cancel her homeowner's policy. With a newborn and just a part-time hairdresser's job, she had lost their house. Instead, she needed renter's insurance for the small apartment she had moved into.

A few months after that she called again. This time it was to cancel the policy on her all-wheel drive vehicle—pretty much a necessity in wintry Wyoming—and replace it with liability-only coverage on a '72 Ford pickup with 500,000 miles on it someone had given her.

I thought I couldn't feel any more miserable until some weeks later when I heard from her one more time. She was canceling all her coverages because she simply couldn't make it on her own anymore. She was heading back to California, to move in with her parents.

That experience continued to eat at me. I beat myself up for not having pushed her husband a little harder to reconsider. I'd think about her from time to time, wondering how she and her children were doing and saying a little prayer for them. A few

A WHOLE LIFE

years later, I tracked her down on social media and asked how things were going.

She told me the situation with her parents hadn't been good, and she had started dating a man she should have known better than to get involved with. They had married, and for several years she had endured a physically and emotionally abusive relationship to try to provide some sort of stability for her children. Eventually, they divorced.

About a year ago, she told me, she had remarried to a guy she met in church, and they were happy and doing well.

I was both grieved and relieved. "I'm glad to hear things are going better for you now, but I want to apologize for what you and your children have been through," I told her. "That's on me."

"What do you mean?" she said.

"Well, if I'd done my job as an insurance agent, your husband would have had a life insurance policy and you wouldn't have felt you had to remarry out of necessity," I said. "I'm so sorry."

She assured me I had nothing to apologize for, but I still felt bad. To this day, her experience prompts me to push for an uncomfortable conversation when it comes to life insurance, and I share her story with other agents to save them from ever having to face the kind of regret I did.

Life insurance is more of an emotional sell than anything, so I am not ashamed to try to touch people's heartstrings by sharing stories like that one. But I start with the facts: I'll tell a couple that around 7,500 people pass away in the United States every day—that's 2.5 million a year. What would they do if one of them were among that number? I will ask. "Imagine you don't make it home tomorrow," I might say to the guy, "what would your wife do?" Then I'll look at her. If he tries to speak, I'll hold up a hand and smile, "Sorry, you don't get to help. You're not here anymore, remember?" They get the point.

I also learned that once you have touched someone's heart, it's important to reach their head. Writing down the pros and cons—even better, having them make the comparison list on a piece of paper themselves, as you talk with them—captures the benefits in unavoidable black and white.

I have always made a point of attending a client's funeral, if possible. I don't make a show of being there, of course, but I believe it is important to be present. First, it's a mark of respect for someone I have done business with. And, I have learned, it's also a small measure of comfort to those who are grieving—a reminder that while their life has changed in ways they would never choose, they have some security as they navigate the difficult days ahead. One time, when I went to offer my condolences to the widow of a client at the end of the service, she took my arm, and introduced me to those around her as "the man who made it possible for us to keep our house." Though it's not my motive for being there, I have come away from funerals with contact details of people who want to talk to me about sorting out their life insurance.

Eleven years after I delivered my last bags of Frito-Lay chips, I was riding high. Through hard work and some thinking outside the box, I had built up an agency that was known and respected throughout the industry. While most Farmers agents carried around 1,200 policies, I had almost four times that number. I had a shelf full of trophies, but more importantly, a heart full of memories. I'd been able to provide for my family all the things I had longed for and more when I was a kid. More meaningful than all the trips and the toys, though, was the love we shared as a family.

Why mess with a good thing? For years, I'd declined invitations to become a district manager and recruit and develop new agents. I knew I wanted to become one at some stage because I saw it as a way to provide opportunities for other people, just like Ken had done for me when he read my sad resume and was intrigued by my church mission reference. The invitations to take over a district had started coming early in my Farmers life, but I felt I needed more experience, so I restricted my mentoring to the presentations and seminars I was asked to do. I loved helping struggling agents get fresh encouragement and new ideas.

Roy Smith, who was president of Farmers' life insurance division, knew that people appreciated my talks, and he wanted to broaden the audience for them. He came to me in 2013 with a proposal: the company wanted to create a new position, head of agent life development. I'd travel around telling my story, lighting a fire under weary or struggling agents, fanning the flames, and providing some fuel in the form of ideas and practices that had worked for me—quite a platform for the kid who once couldn't speak clearly enough for people to understand.

It was an exciting opportunity because, much as I loved selling insurance, I enjoyed teaching about it even more. And I felt like I could help more clients indirectly by sharing some of what I had learned with other agents, multiplying my impact. However, it would mean selling my agency and leaving the security of what I had built up for the unknown.

Kim could see how much the invitation meant to me and encouraged me to go for it. I traveled extensively for the next three years, training and equipping agents nationwide. As when I'd first started with Farmers, Kim quietly carried the burden of ensuring our home and family life ran well without complaining.

It was an exciting and rewarding season. Almost everywhere I went, agents' numbers went up after I spoke. It was rewarding to have them come up to me after a session and tell me that I had inspired them to keep going. But I always knew that this gig was only for a period. I didn't want to be one of those experts who went around telling everyone else how to do a job he hadn't actually practiced for years.

I also felt that I was now ready to finally become a district manager. I'd been approached about many different opportunities as I traveled around and turned them down. When I hung up my head of agent life development hat, I had twelve district manager offers on my desk.

I chose Fort Collins, Colorado, for several reasons. It was only three hours from Casper, where our grown children were establishing their own lives, so we could still get to see them frequently. It was also a beautiful part of the country with a special place in our hearts—as the kids were growing up, we'd often gone there for mini-breakaways. Plus, business-wise, it was struggling, which made it ripe for improvement. It appealed to my spirit of adventure. It would be like starting from scratch again, in some ways. I hit the ground running, and by the end of my first year, we had more than doubled our target numbers. In my first year as a district manager, we finished second in life insurance nationwide.

Once again, life was good, and I thought I would retire from my district manager's role at some stage. What made it even more rewarding was having some of my children join me as part of the team of thirty agents and associates. But being a district manager was pretty much all-consuming. Though I did not want to continue speaking full-time as I had done, I did still enjoy being able to impart to other agents occasionally, and I just didn't have the time to do it anymore.

So, after six years, I made another leap of faith. Leaving Farmers, I went out as an independent agent for the first time. While I knew I would have to work hard to build up a new business from scratch, I could draw on some of the best practices I had learned through the years. Avoiding some of the mistakes and not-so-successful things I had tried earlier would free up time for me to do some more speaking, too.

The last few years have been challenging but also a lot of fun, as I have gotten to do this with several of my family members as part of the team. Starting out again has also reminded me about the danger of coasting, getting to a certain level, and then sitting back and taking your foot off the gas pedal. As an independent agent, you have to work harder for new business—there's no corporate funnel of inquiries.

Starting over, I have also had to learn some new skills and new tricks. The COVID-19 pandemic that locked us all in our homes for a season permanently changed the way many of us do business and life. Most of my sales used to be made in person because that sense of personal connection was so important, but nowadays the majority of my work is done remotely. People have gotten comfortable, or at least more used to, connecting online. While the virtual world has made everything a little more functional, it's still important to try to establish some kind of relationship, of course, so I will look for clues if we're Zooming; maybe there's something behind them—a book or a photograph or a piece of artwork—that can spark a question or a comment.

Social media has become another sales channel. It brings me into contact with people all over the country, so I have my life insurance license in thirty-six states, to be able to service clients there. It's a worthwhile investment.

> ONE THING I AM CERTAIN OF IS THAT WHATEVER HARDSHIPS WE FACE, THEY DON'T HAVE TO DEFINE US.

Online, I share stories from time to time about how insurance has helped some of my clients, with their permission. But I don't just talk business. After all, it's called social media. So, I also set out to be simply social, friendly—I'll post "this or that" questions, asking people to choose between, say, two bands or two fast-food chains. The aim is to have people interact with me somehow. And if they do, I always make a point to at least acknowledge their comment. If they can take the time to post in response to something I have said, it's rude not to recognize that. It's amazing how many times someone will reach out to me to discuss insurance because they feel like they know me a little through my Facebook posts.

Some of the ways of doing business may have changed, but the challenge remains the same. I greet every day as an adventure to be enjoyed. Who knows what the next call or appointment may bring? One thing I am certain of is that whatever hardships we face, they don't have to define us. With trust in God, a positive attitude, and a determination to do our best, we can experience a life of purpose and satisfaction.

> **WITH TRUST IN GOD, A POSITIVE ATTITUDE, AND A DETERMINATION TO DO OUR BEST, WE CAN EXPERIENCE A LIFE OF PURPOSE AND SATISFACTION.**

AFTERWORD

When people hear a little of my story, they sometimes ask me how I came through so apparently unscathed. What lessons about surviving difficult times and overcoming adversity might I have for others? I wish I had a really good answer—apart from anything else, if I could bottle it for sale, I'd be a multimillionaire—but I don't.

First, I recognize that there are people who have endured far worse things than I did. Yes, I suffered some neglect, but it was more by default than deliberate, in a sense. I was never chained to a radiator or beaten, like you read about in some people's life stories. I don't think anyone set out intentionally to be unkind to me; they were just more focused on their own wants and needs, and my well-being was secondary. Though I suffered to a degree as a result, I'm able to be forgiving.

I have in mind one of my favorite quotes from one of my favorite movies of all time, the prison drama *The Shawshank Redemption*. Jailed for life for a crime he didn't commit, Andy Dufresne tries to make the best of his situation and tells a fellow inmate, "I guess it comes down to a simple choice, really. Get busy living or get busy dying."[31]

---

[31] Frank Darabont, *The Shawshank Redemption* (September 10, 1994; Beverly Hills, CA: Castle Rock Entertainment).

A WHOLE LIFE

That's been my attitude. Sitting around feeling sorry for myself isn't going to get me anywhere. I can't change what happened in the past, however much I might want to. But I don't have to let it limit how I live now or keep me from having a brighter future. Life may have been hard back then, but I can choose to make it good now. It's all about where I focus my attention. As Dale Carnegie said, "Two men looked out from prison bars. One saw the mud, the other saw stars."[32] From being young, rather than dwelling on the downside, I decided to try to find the positive in things. Okay, I didn't have those new clothes or that bicycle for long, but they gave me a glimpse of what could be mine. And I could still walk to the Fireside Rec to have some fun.

While some of the things I experienced have left me tenderhearted toward those who go through difficult times, they also helped toughen me up in a good way. I learned to be resilient. There comes a point in the game of life when you have to decide whether you are going to play the cards you have been given or fold.

I have also been asked whether I would go back and change anything if I could. My answer: no. I'm not saying I am glad for what happened, but I am glad for how things turned out. Those experiences were all part of shaping and forming me into the person I am today—and I like him! They taught me about people and how the world works. The Bible says that "in all things God

---

32 Dale Carnegie, "Two men looked out from prison bars; one saw the mud, the other saw stars," *Quotefancy*, https://quotefancy.com/quote/47109/Dale-Carnegie-Two-men-looked-out-from-prison-bars-One-saw-the-mud-the-other-saw-stars.

works for the good of those who love him, who have been called according to his purpose" (Romans 8:28, NIV), and I believe that. My faith has certainly been an essential factor. I have little doubt that if God had not intervened as He did, I would have probably ended up lost in addiction, locked up, or dead, just like so many others in my family. I am so grateful for His tremendous love and mercy. Sometimes, I almost feel a little guilty: how did I get to experience His grace and goodness and they didn't? It can seem unfair.

The reality is, I don't know what happened in their lives. But I do believe this: God is absolutely good and entirely fair, and when He made us, He gave us free will to make our own choices. He may have put His hand out to them, and they may have chosen not to receive it. One day, I'll get the answer, but for now, I have to leave them with Him and trust Him with them.

> **GOD IS ABSOLUTELY GOOD AND ENTIRELY FAIR, AND WHEN HE MADE US, HE GAVE US FREE WILL TO MAKE OUR OWN CHOICES.**

I like to think that in making me who I am, my past also benefits others. It has made me sensitive to those going through hard times, and I want to help out as and where I can. I know part of the reason I've loved selling life insurance is that it provides people with security—something I lacked often—that has helped them through hard times. And if I can help someone, who knows what kind of ripple effect that might have if it encourages them to help someone else? I think back to how people like Frank, sharing his chicken pot pie with me at the Fireside Rec, where Bill befriended me, made such an impact on me. Small acts of kindness can snowball. It's like George Bailey in *It's a Wonderful Life*[33]: we never know what effect we can have on the people around us.

Sharing my experiences has helped people, too. I don't go into many details when talking to insurance groups, but I tell folks a little about overcoming hard times. I talk about growing up in challenging circumstances, looking for comfort and meaning in the wrong places, dealing with addiction, and how my life turned around when I found God. I tell them that any success I've had is because my priorities have been God, family, work, in that order. It's surprising how many people come to me afterward to thank me for being so honest. It is so satisfying to hear them say things like, "You didn't only make me want to sell more insurance; you made me want to be a better person."

After one presentation, a woman came up to me with tears in her eyes. She told me that she was pretty new to the insurance world and that she was having a hard time making a go of it. She hadn't planned to attend the event I was speaking at because it was pretty expensive for her, but something inside had told her she needed to be there. On the way to the venue, she had a flat and almost decided to give up and go home. But she felt that small voice nagging her.

---

33 Frank Capra, *It's a Wonderful Life* (December 20, 1946; Los Angeles, CA: Liberty Films).

"I'm so glad I listened to it," she told me. "What you've taught me today is about so much more than just insurance." She confided that she was a recovering meth addict. "I've been clean for a couple of years, but there are things going on in my life right now that are making me want to go back to that old world," she said. "Hearing you talk about being addicted to things and how you found God and have changed your life has made me realize I can do this."

People often talk about "closure" to painful episodes, but I don't believe that's always possible. Some things can't be tied up in a nice, neat bow; there are times when you have to let them be and move on with your life.

That's been the case with my family. I realize that I may never know the whole story, and that's okay. Looking for answers can lead to even more obscure questions. For example, take trying to find out more about my dad. It was helpful to unearth some independent evidence online about his criminal past. Not that I felt good about it, but it confirmed some of the reputation he had in the family. Discovering he fathered at least two half-siblings was bittersweet, but I decided not to pursue that breadcrumb trail. Both of them have passed, so it's not like I am ever going to be able to have a relationship with them. Then there's the question mark over his marriage to Mom. While I found a record of his previous marriage, I discovered no details of his and Mom's wedding or divorce. Maybe that information is out there somewhere, or perhaps they never actually tied the knot. If not, that might explain why I wasn't given his last name before Royce adopted me and I became a Jameson.

A WHOLE LIFE

That is a question I may get to ask Mom one day, although I am not holding my breath. We haven't spoken for several years now. I tried to maintain some sort of relationship for a long time, but it was challenging. At one stage, when she was having a hard time, we invited her to move up and live near us in Casper. We helped her get situated with an apartment, and I was excited that because she was now close to us, she would be able to celebrate a family birthday in person for the first time. But on the day of our son Mark's fifth birthday, she told me she wouldn't be coming to his party: she wanted to go to a gun show with her neighbor instead because it would be more fun.

Not surprisingly, the Casper move didn't last long, but I kept in contact occasionally. Part of me was still hoping to hear some words of affirmation that she was proud of what I had achieved. But they never came; each time I hung up the phone after speaking with her, I'd feel depressed. Eventually, Kim wisely advised that I needed to let things go, not only for my own well-being but for how my mood would affect the rest of the family for a while until I bounced back.

And if Mom ever reads this? Well, I have tried to be clear about my story but not cruel. I hope that she sees my ongoing love for her despite everything. For all the ways I feel I didn't get everything I needed from her, I remind myself of this: I and my half-siblings did all get life. Other women in similar situations may have made different choices upon learning they were pregnant. Above all, I hope she might one day discover what I have found—God's forgiveness, freedom, and faithfulness.

The same is true for my surviving half-siblings. After learning about Jeffrey, Tracy tracked him down on social media and asked me whether I wanted her to connect me with him. I said no, though I did seek him out online and saw an undeniable family resemblance in his photo. But while I wish him well, I don't feel the need to try to create a relationship that is tenuous at best.

I kept in touch with Cheryl and Tracy for many years. I remain deeply grateful to Cheryl for her care of me even when she was going through her own difficulties in the family; later, she came and lived with us for a while at one stage, which made me feel I was able to repay some measure of all her kindness to me when I was young. And I continued to feel protective toward Tracy, who faced her own situations. However, I've had to let those relationships go, too, for now. Over time, it began to feel like they only made contact when they needed some kind of help, and, much as I was glad to offer it at first, it wasn't the best thing to keep doing. There is a fine line between helping and enabling, and I also had a growing family of my own I needed to focus on.

Though I've never needed professional help and enjoyed a lot of success, I don't want to give the impression that my life has been all sunbeams and rainbows. As I mentioned, even with a healthy measure of determination, there have been times when I have doubted myself. I'm grateful every day for Kim and her faithfulness and steadfastness. Others have been an encouragement and inspiration to me along the way—notably, Kim's father, who, in many ways, became the dad I'd never had. We called each other "Dad" and "son."

And there have been challenges. I don't think any parent sees their children grow into adulthood without some bumps and bruises along the way. I'm blessed to have a great relationship with all five of my kids, four of whom are part of the business (along with a son-in-law), but there have been some hard times.

Going through those things despite Kim's and my best efforts as parents reminds me that life is about both nurture and nature—not only the environment in which we grow up but the genes we inherit. If addiction was like a fault line running through my family, then so were mental health issues. That's no surprise because the two are often inextricably intertwined. I'm no expert, but it seems to me they can be like the old chicken and the egg problem: which comes first? People struggling with mental health problems can look to alcohol and drugs as a way of self-medicating, while in turn, getting high and wasted can damage your brain. I wonder how much of the way people in the family acted was because of undiagnosed mental health issues. After all, this was in a time when it was less understood and certainly less talked about. It's not hard to see evidence of bipolar disorder and even schizophrenia.

> **LIFE IS ABOUT BOTH NURTURE AND NATURE—NOT ONLY THE ENVIRONMENT IN WHICH WE GROW UP BUT THE GENES WE INHERIT.**

I'm so thankful that while I struggled with addiction for a time, I never got sucked into its darkest corners. I always steered clear of hard drugs, in part because of what I saw them do in my family, like the way they affected Garry and Jack and other relatives.

I'm also grateful that, other than for that one episode when I was in Dallas and found myself despairing, I seem to have escaped the tentacles of suicide that wrapped themselves around some family members.

There was Garry, of course. My sadness that he had felt so hopeless was heightened by a suspicion that part of the reason he took his own life was because he didn't want to be a burden to others anymore. Beneath the craziness of some of his behaviors was still the kind, sensitive kid I had known when he was younger. Then there was my cousin William, who never got over Bobby Joe's death.

Suicide came even closer to me than I knew for a long time. In a rare candid conversation Mom and I had one time when I was an adult, she talked a little about how difficult things had been for her after my dad had gone to prison, and she was bringing me and the others up alone. One day, with no food and no money in the house, Mom had gotten utterly overwhelmed. She turned the gas on in the house as we slept, intending to end things. The sound of kids playing somewhere outside had jolted her back into reality, she told me. She got up and turned the stove off. That's another choice of hers I am grateful for.

Though I seem to have dodged it, I can see clearly how many of my family were affected by mental health troubles, back when there was less awareness and less help available. It gives me a measure more of sympathy for why they did and said some of what they did.

At the same time, I don't believe that absolves people of all responsibility for their actions and how they affect others. I'm just thankful that from that day I opened the door to those two young women on a church mission, I have never felt the desire to fill the emptiness that was inside of me with some external stimulant. I put that down to God's hand on my life, for which I remain always grateful. And I believe that same help is available to all of us—it's just a prayer away.

ABOUT THE AUTHOR

Jack Jameson is one of the insurance industry's top-performing agents and an in-demand trainer and motivational speaker.

During twenty years with Farmers, he received multiple awards and honors, in addition to being selected for the President's Council for the top 0.5 percent of agents for seven years. He was also a qualifying member of the Million Dollar Round Table for six consecutive years.

For three years, Jack served as Head of Agent Life Development for Farmers New World Life, speaking to agents across the United States. He was a Farmers district manager for several years, before starting his independent agency, JWR Insurance Group, in 2022.

Jack continues to travel and speak, inspiring and equipping other agents. He also offers training through his personal Jack's 2 Life Crew and Jack's Life College online groups.

Jack and his wife, Kim, have been married for thirty-five years and make their home in Fort Collins, Colorado. They have five children and seven grandchildren. A die-hard Dallas Cowboys, Texas Rangers, and LSU Tigers fan, he enjoys sports and spending time with his family.

FIND OUT MORE AND FOLLOW JACK AT:

▶ @jackjameson4life

🌐 www.jackjameson.life

ⓕ jack.jameson.942

in jack-jameson-8a917a9b

FOR SPEAKING INVITATIONS, CONTACT:

✉ Jackj@jacks2lifecrew.com
(307) 247-1519

www.ingramcontent.com/pod-product-compliance
Lightning Source LLC
Chambersburg PA
CBHW070533090426
42735CB00013B/2964